Marita Knobel • Brigitte Steinert

**Singing Opera in Germany**

## About the Authors

**Marita Knobel** was born in Johannesburg, South Africa, and studied psychology, voice pathology and speech therapy at the University of Pretoria. She worked subsequently for six years as a speech therapist for disabled children while singing in her free time at the Pretoria State Opera. After completing her studies at the London Opera Centre, she began her career as a soloist (mezzo-soprano) at the Cologne City Opera, in Germany in 1971. There she sang many roles of her *Fach*, specializing in the German, Slavic and modern repertoire. Fourteen years later she returned to South Africa as Assistant Artistic Director at the Cape Town Opera, where she also developed the Young Professionals Training Program.
In 1985 she resumed her operatic career in Germany, where after a few years of freelancing she joined the Bavarian State Opera in Munich as a soloist in the character *Fach*. She has also appeared as a guest singer in Barcelona, Madrid, Bilbao, Rome, Tokyo, Vienna, Tel Aviv, Strasbourg and Toulouse.
Marita Knobel now offers individual audition training and career counselling for the operatic profession. She is also the founder and artistic director of the *Sommerkurs für Operndarstellung*, a summer course offering movement, acting, musical interpretation and audition training in Munich.
She is the co-author of the German opera handbook, *Beruf: Opernsänger. Ein Ratgeber*, which was published by Bärenreiter in 2002.

**Brigitte Steinert** is the chief librarian of a Bavarian state cultural institution and is a qualified cultural manager. She studied singing with *Kammersänger* Karl Christian Kohn and stage direction with Horst Reday at the *Richard-Strauss-Konservatorium* in Munich. She sang for ten years in the extra chorus of the Bavarian State Opera and was a soloist and assistant stage director at the *Freies Landestheater Bayern*.
She does audition training, career counselling and German dialogue for the stage. She is the co-director of the *Sommerkurs für Operndarstellung* and founding chairman of the *Förderverein Meisterkurse für Operndarstellung e.V.* in Munich.
She is the co-author of *Beruf: Opernsänger*.

Marita Knobel • Brigitte Steinert

# Singing Opera in Germany

A Practical Guide

Bärenreiter
Kassel • Basel • London • New York • Prag

Bibliographic information published by Die Deutsche Bibliothek
Die Deutsche Bibliothek lists this publication in the Deutsche
Nationalbibliografie: detailed bibliographic data is available
in the internet at http://dnb.ddb.de.


www.baerenreiter.com


© 2005 Bärenreiter-Verlag Karl Vötterle GmbH & Co. KG, Kassel
Translated, Revised and Enlarged Edition of Marita Knobel/
Brigitte Steinert: *Beruf: Opernsänger. Ein Ratgeber*, Kassel: Bären-
reiter-Verlag, 2002
Cover: Marita Knobel (Nutrice) and Nadja Michael (Ottavia) in:
L'incoronazione di Poppea, Production: David Alden, Bayerische
Staatsoper 1997
Cover design: Jörg Richter, Bad Emstal-Sand
Editors: Jutta Schmoll-Barthel/Diana Rothaug
Design and Typeset: Dorothea Willerding
Printed in Germany: Druckhaus »Thomas Müntzer«,
Bad Langensalza
ISBN 3-7618-1673-1

# Contents

## Appendix

## Foreword

This book is based on our handbook for young opera singers, *Beruf Opernsänger*, which was published in Germany in 2002. The English version is intended to help young opera singers from other countries to make a career in Germany. Many of our readers who are at the beginning of their careers live in countries or areas where there are no opera houses or opera schools and they consequently lack experience in the opera business. Although you can't learn acting and singing out of a book, we have also included some basic information on these subjects.

In the past, Germany was Utopia for opera singers from all over the world. Within the last five years however, the situation has changed dramatically. The global economic situation plus the specific financial problems created by the reunification of East and West Germany have forced many opera houses to close down or tighten their budgets. This has resulted in a reduction of the amount of vacancies available every year. The reality is that you may find 200 singers lining up for one solitary vacancy within a single week. The opera houses are at present in the enviable position of having the pick of the bunch.

This handbook is intended to give you the know-how on what to do and what not to do in order to achieve your goal. We hope that it will be read by young singers in Great Britain, the United States, Canada, Australia, New Zealand and Africa as well as South America and the Asian countries.

A few hints for using this book:
* Our book addresses the specific situation in Germany, but many of the facts can also be applied to opera houses in Austria and Switzerland, which function along the same lines.
* The German expressions in brackets are in the nominative singular form.

* We use British English.
* We use the male form when referring to somebody. This is done for practical purposes. We are well aware of the fact that people working in the opera business can always be male and female.

Dear aspiring opera singers – a word of advice on your way: You will be moving into a career packed with rich traditions that have a very long historical background and comprise a magnificent artistic treasure. There is much to learn, much more than you can even begin to anticipate at the start. It will take time and effort to grow into becoming a complete singer-actor. Do not expect that what you bring into this profession – your enthusiasm, natural talent and lovely voice – is going to be good enough by itself. Dedicated opera singers never stop learning until the day they retire from this wonderful but extremely complex profession.
Our aim is to encourage the most talented singers before they start out on the exciting journey of becoming an opera singer in Germany. We also hope to discourage those singers who do not belong on the opera stage.

We wish to thank Roger Clement for his support and Jennifer Trost, Assistant Professor of Singing at the Pennsylvania State University for her professional advice.
A special thanks to our friend, Neville Dove, Senior Coach and Rehearsal Conductor at the Bavarian State Opera, for his invaluable advice and support.
We wish you all a hearty toi-toi-toi!*

Munich, March 2005
The Authors

* Toi-toi-toi means good luck, and is used universally by theatre people in German-speaking countries. It originated from the tradition of spitting three times over the left shoulder of your colleague.

# When in Germany, do as the Germans do

## Does the typical German really exist?

The following (from www.campus-germany.de) was written by the Romanian-born student Ana-Maria Tighineanu, living in Germany since 1999:
"Germans drink beer at the Oktoberfest, in lederhosen and a silly hat. Proper Germans are blond and have blue eyes. They live on sausages with sauerkraut. And their music does not go beyond Beethoven and Bach. Clichés abound. Always good for a laugh when you try to find an answer for what is typically German. But what is typical, when you are talking about a country with a population of more than 80 million?"
To answer this question, we will start with some background in German geography and history.

### Federal States
The Federal Republic of Germany (*die Bundesrepublik Deutschland*) consists of 16 Federal States (*das Bundesland*) and – believe it or not – these states and their inhabitants are so different from each other that even the Germans themselves are surprised at how big these differences are.

On 9 November 1989, the most important historical and political event since the Second World War occurred in Germany. With the fall of the Berlin Wall, the reunification of the two German countries became possible. After a year of negotiation, East Germany, the former communist German Democratic Republic with its states Mecklenburg-Vorpommern, Brandenburg, Sachsen, Thüringen and Sachsen-Anhalt, joined the democratic Federal Republic of Germany on 3 October 1990.

# 1 • When in Germany, do as the Germans do

| Federal States | Capital Cities |
|---|---|
| Baden-Württemberg | Stuttgart |
| Bayern | München |
| Berlin | Berlin |
| Brandenburg | Potsdam |
| Bremen | Bremen |
| Hamburg | Hamburg |
| Hessen | Wiesbaden |
| Mecklenburg-Vorpommern | Schwerin |
| Niedersachen | Hannover |
| Nordrhein-Westfalen | Düsseldorf |
| Rheinland-Pfalz | Mainz |
| Saarland | Saarbrücken |
| Sachsen | Dresden |
| Sachsen-Anhalt | Magdeburg |
| Schleswig-Holstein | Kiel |
| Thüringen | Erfurt |

The difficulties arising from the personal, political, economical and social coming-together of two different population groups have still not been fully resolved. The former East Germans grew up in a totalitarian system and have had to adjust to capitalism in a very short time. There are still some differences between East and West Germans, as well as the usual regional differences that are normal in a country with so long a history, such as:

♦ The geographical differences between the Alps in the south and the sea in the north.

♦ The climate, which can be rough in the coastal and mountain areas, yet mild in the wine-growing areas in the west and south-west. You will be surprised to find that people in the wine-growing regions are more outgoing than people living in the beer-brewing areas.

♦ The difference between the conservative life in the country, and the big cities where people are more open-minded and used to living in a multicultural society.

12

* The variety of dialects, which are sometimes hard even for a German to understand.

This is only a small and incomplete list. When you come to Germany you will find many more. Be prepared! There is no such thing as "the typical German".
There are, nevertheless, a few typical habits you should be aware of if you want to become a successful guest or inhabitant of this interesting and diverse country.
The following tips should make your stay easier and more pleasant.

## Daily life

For general information on the city, town or village you will live in look up its website. There you will find useful information on the town and the surrounding area. The website of Munich (*München*) for instance would be www.muenchen.de (*ä, ö* or *ü* have to be changed to *ae, oe* or *ue* in the web).

**Public transport**

Public transport is very efficient in Germany, in the big cities as well as the smaller towns. It will not be necessary to own a car. You will be able to rely on the time-tables for trains, busses, underground (subway) and trams. It is possible to buy weekly or monthly tickets in advance. These are much cheaper than single tickets.

**Driver's licence**

If you plan to stay longer, you should get your driver's licence changed into a valid German one as soon as possible. This can only be done within the first few months of your stay. After that, you will have to apply for a German licence, with all the necessary tests. This can prove difficult and very expensive. For further information see www.verkehrsportal.de (in German) or go to the local office of the German automobile club (*der Allgemeine Deutsche Automobilclub*, abbr. *ADAC*).

# 1 • When in Germany, do as the Germans do

**24-hour clock**

In Germany, one uses the 24-hour clock. A train will depart at 13.00 (1:00 p.m.) and arrive at 16.10 (4:10 p.m.). Your first rehearsal of the day will start at 10.00 in the morning and could end at 13.00 (1:00 p.m.). Your afternoon rehearsal might start at 17.00 (5:00 p.m.) and end at 21.00 (9:00 p.m.). Midnight is at 24.00 also called 0.00.

**Accommodation**

It is not always easy to find suitable and cheap accommodation, particularly in the big cities. Your first step should be to find a furnished place to stay for a couple of months. Websites like www.homecompany.de or www.mitwohnzentrale.de will be helpful here. You could also try www.immonet.de if your German is good enough. Once you are on the spot it will be easier to find a place to rent. You can then advertize or read the rent notices in the local newspaper and look at the notice board in the theatre or (for students) in the university. Students should also contact the student union (*das Studentenwerk*) of the university. You'll find it in the university website.

Once you have decided to live in Germany and have found a place to stay (*der Wohnsitz*), the first thing to do is to register (*die Anmeldung*) with the authorities. When you change addresses, you have to cancel (*abmelden*) your registration and re-register the new address.

**Tip**

An apartment (*das Appartement*) in Germany is a bed-sitter with normally only one room.

**Shopping**

Department stores are usually open Monday through Saturday from 9.30 to 20.00. Smaller shops and bakeries open earlier in the morning, some as early as 7.00, but then will close by 18.00. On Sundays all shops are closed except for a few bakeries and florists in the morning and the very expensive supermarkets in the main train stations. If you see supermarkets named ALDI, PLUS, PENNY, NORMA or LIDL you can be assured of low prices and good quality.

**Tip**

The Germans are very aware of environmental pollution (*die Umweltverschmutzung*) and many shoppers will look at you with disapproval if you ask for a plastic shopping bag. We suggest that you always carry a cloth shopping bag.

## Weights and quantities

Whether you're shopping or reading a recipe – welcome to the land of the kilogram (*das Kilogramm* or *Kilo,* abbr. *kg*), the gram (*das Gramm,* abbr. *g*), the litre (*der Liter,* abbr. *l*) and the millilitre (*der Milliliter,* abbr. *ml*).

For quick conversion of kilograms into pounds, use the following formula: double the kilogram weight and then add 10%. Example: 50 kilos × 2 = 100 + 10% = 110 lbs.

1 kg = 1,000 g
The word pound (*das Pfund*) is often used in the south.
1 Pfund = 500 g = ½ kg (not to be confused with the English pound!)
1 l = 1,000 ml (1 quart is slightly less than 1 litre)

## Linear measurement

The linear measurements are the kilometre (*der Kilometer,* abbr. *km*), the metre (*der Meter,* abbr. *m*), the centimetre (*der Centimeter,* abbr. *cm*) and the millimetre (*der Millimeter,* abbr. *mm*).

1 km = 1,000 m; 1 m = 100 cm; 1 cm = 10 mm
0.39 inches = 1 cm; 1 foot = 30.5 cm; 1 yard = 91.5 cm;
1 mile = 1.6 km

In Germany, one writes divisions with commas instead of full-stops (periods): 1,6 km instead of 1.6 km.

Tip

## Temperature

Temperature is measured in Celsius
0° Celsius = 32° Fahrenheit (freezing point)
17.8° Celsius = 0° Fahrenheit
20° Celsius = 68° Fahrenheit (room temperature)
100° Celsius = 212° Fahrenheit (boiling)
In German, you say 20 *Grad* without the word "Celsius".

Normal body temperature is 37 *Grad.* A temperature above normal begins at 38 *Grad.* A high temperature is between 39 and 41 *Grad.*

# I ◆ When in Germany, do as the Germans do

**Electricity**

The standard electric current in Germany is 220 volts. You might need a transformer for your appliances, depending on where you come from.

**Health care and pharmacies (chemists)**

In Germany you will find many general practitioners (*der Allgemeinarzt/die Allgemeinärztin*). It makes sense to go to a GP first who will then recommend the necessary specialists. To find a good dentist (*der Zahnarzt/die Zahnärztin*) ask your colleagues or friends for a recommendation.

Medicine, with or without prescription, can only be bought in a pharmacy or a chemist (*die Apotheke*). You won't find medication in a normal supermarket or drugstore (*die Drogerie*). You will find vitamin pills there, but to get quality vitamins we suggest you ask your pharmacist or chemist.

In general, your health insurance will pay for a normal check-up by your GP, also for treatment by a specialist, for hospital treatment, for all prescription drugs, or for certain dental work. Specialized dental work such as crowns, bridges or dentures are not covered completely. You should explore the possibilities of additional insurance to cover these extra costs (see chapter 6).

**Tip**

The medication you have been taking at home will have a different name in Germany. It might be a good idea to find out from your doctor at home what the exact ingredients of your regular medication are, so that you will be able to find it in Germany.

**Banking**

The first thing to do after arriving in Germany is to open a bank account (*das Girokonto*). Ask your bank to explain to you how to do automatic monthly transfers (*der Dauerauftrag*) for your rent (*die Miete*) and utilities like electricity, gas, water and telephone. In Germany, most money transactions are done by bank transfers (this can also be done online) and not by cheque as is usual in some other countries (see p. 104f.).

Smoking is allowed in most restaurants and also in theatre canteens (cafeterias) at certain times. If you want to avoid smokers, look for signs saying *Rauchen Verboten* (No Smoking) or *Nichtraucherzone* (non-smoking zone). Smoking is not allowed in trams, busses and undergrounds (subways). On the national and international trains you will find special smoking compartments.

**Smoking**

In Germany you have to pay a monthly fee to the *GEZ* (*die Gebühreneinzugszentrale*) if you own a radio or a television set. You must go to the Post Office or your bank to register for this. Controllers come around regularly to check, and if you are caught without a subscription, you have to pay quite a big fine. This also applies to your car radio.

**Television and radio**

If you call someone you don't know very well, you should announce yourself by giving your full name. If the person you need to speak to does not answer personally and you have to ask for him or her, it will be regarded as impolite not to identify yourself first.

In Germany it is normal practice to answer your own phone with your surname. This may sound very formal and odd to people who come from countries where one just says "hello", but, when in Germany, do as the Germans do. It will make a bad impression on a business partner not to follow this custom.

A cell phone or mobile phone is called *das Handy* in German.

**Telephoning**

Police: 110
Fire Station or Ambulance: 112

**Important telephone numbers**

Another typical quality of German life is punctuality. If you get an invitation for 19.00, be there at 7:00 p.m. (remember the 24-hour clock). You should never arrive late, but don't come too early, either. It is customary to bring a small gift, such as flowers or chocolates for the hostess. For the host, a good bottle of wine will always be welcome.

**Punctuality**

# I • When in Germany, do as the Germans do

**Weather**

Your rule-of-thumb is: Be prepared for warm, cold and very cold days in each season. Don't be fooled by the word 'summer'! Summer in Germany very often turns out to be cold, windy and rainy, but it can also become very hot and humid. For summer, bring a warm sweater, an outdoor jacket, summer clothes, and don't forget your umbrella! Autumn (fall) and spring can surprise you with real summer days and temperatures around 25°C (77°F). But the next day can be rainy and stormy! Be prepared for snow and ice in winter. You should bring a good pair of waterproof boots with thick soles, warm gloves, a scarf and a warm hat.

**Seasons**

Spring: March, April, May (*März, April, Mai*);
Summer: June, July, August (*Juni, Juli, August*);
Autumn: September, October, November (*September, Oktober, November*);
Winter: December, January, February (*Dezember, Januar, Februar*).

**What to wear**

In general, Germans do not overdress. The well-dressed woman doesn't use too much make-up and jewellery. Strong perfume during the day will be regarded as slightly common. Understatement is considered chic at any time of the day. You will also see the opposite, but this is not really considered suitable for the singing profession. The days of the divas dripping in furs and jewellery are over. This does not mean that one should be sloppy. Chic but understated is the rule. For men, blazers and jackets are worn far more commonly than in other countries, but it will be acceptable to replace a formal shirt with a good quality T-shirt.

## Privacy, friends, "Du" or "Sie" and more ...

The Germans like their privacy. The German word for this is *die Privatsphäre* and you will quickly find out how important this is. It is not a good idea to pay an unannounced visit to anyone who is not a close friend.

**Acquaintances or friends?**

For a German, a friend is someone to whom he or she is very close. You can trust such a friend in all situations, and these friendships normally last for a lifetime. Maybe this sounds a little bit over the top, but there are advantages to having a few good friends and keeping the others at a slight distance. This will inevitably include your superiors as well as certain colleagues.

**Forms of speech**

In your first German lessons you will learn about the difference between the formal *Sie* and the informal *Du* forms of speech. Never use the informal *Du* to a person you don't know well. This can be your boss, landlord, the sales assistant, your doctor or caretaker. You also do not use *Du* when speaking to an older person unless he or she formally offers you the *Du* (*das Du anbieten*). In the theatre, you will find that your colleagues will be far less formal and that you will very soon say *Du* to them, with the exception of the *Intendant* or the GMD (*der Generalmusikdirektor*). It is also a good idea at least in the beginning, to say *Sie* to the stage director (*der Regisseur*).

**Form of address**

A person is addressed as Mr. (*Herr*) or Mrs. (*Frau*) followed by the surname. The term Miss (*Fräulein*) is no longer used in German. It would be considered impolite to address a woman as *Fräulein* privately or otherwise, even if she is not married. The term Ms. does not have a German equivalent. A celebrity will be called *Frau* Kathleen Battle and not *Fräulein* Kathleen Battle.

A 1994 study by the Humboldt Foundation (www.humboldt-foundation.de) revealed the following opinions: " 'typically German' are orderliness, efficiency, discipline, obedience to rules and regulations but also friendliness, openness, helpfulness, and interest in guests. Particular mention is also made of politeness, reliability, a sense of responsibility and

**19**

duty, including to the environment, and preservation of traditional values. Other 'typically German' qualities are said to be reserve, coolness, difficulty in making friends, and a lack of spontaneity. Arrogance, hostility to children and foreigners, egoism, Eurocentrism and a marked inclination to material values are also listed.

When you come to Germany for the first time you might feel strange and sometimes a bit lonely. Meet fellow countrymen to share your experiences but don't forget to make contact with the Germans. People who understand the manner of thought and the everyday life in Germany will be able to help you analyze the difficult task of becoming a part of the German way of life. And the most important advice is: Learn German!

Typical characteristics should apply to a nation as a whole, but are often the result of experience of individuals. You will find that Germans may, indeed, possess the above characteristics, but that the individual character traits of the new colleagues, friends, and acquaintances you make during your stay in Germany will have a more lasting effect on your picture of 'the Germans' than the general impressions made by people as a whole.

However, in spite of the diversity of individual characters, there are distinct cultural and – more particularly – linguistic differences (dialects) in the individual federal states. Depending on the region, people are said to have very special peculiarities and modes of behaviour. Indeed, much of this is based on prejudice but some of it is confirmed now and again.

It is best to trust your own judgement and not be put off by other people's generalizations."

We hope that this chapter will make for better understanding and communication and that you will discover the advantages of living, studying and working in this country with its centuries-old cultural traditions.

**2**

# Studying in Germany

## General requirements

Opera singing is a multi-dimensional art form consisting of singing, acting, speaking and dancing. Before you start your studies, you have to be very aware that each of these facets of stage art is equally important. It is never enough to learn singing technique and hope that the rest will develop by itself. If you feel that your music or opera school does not put enough emphasis on all the facets of singing onstage, you will have to find possibilities of training the lacking skills. The more qualifications and experience you have before coming to Germany the better.

**Are you ready for going abroad?**

It is not such a good idea to go abroad as a nineteen or twenty-year-old "youngster". You will need strength, courage and humour to survive Good Old Europe, and perhaps a strong and supportive partner at your side helping you deal with disorientation and homesickness. It is up to you to decide whether you are ready to take such a major step in your life. You should start studying in your native country and – having gained more experience – go abroad one or two years later to further your studies.

**Advantages to studying in Germany**

Although the opera courses in Germany are not always ideal (as well as all over the world we suppose), there are a few very important advantages to studying in Germany, if you intend on starting a career in Europe:
* You will get to know the singing business in Germany
* You will learn to speak the language fluently
* The tuition is free
* You can compare your skills with other students
* You get to see opera in Germany

# 2 • Studying in Germany

## The first step

**Choosing the school**

There are 23 music schools in Germany. They are called *Musikhochschulen* or *Musikuniversitäten*. The requirements and the details for the application vary from school to school. Therefore it is very important to be well informed. For updated information, look up the schools' websites and ask your friends who have already studied in Germany. You will find a list of music schools and addresses at www.rektorenkonferenz.de. You should compare the programmes that the various music schools offer.

What you learn at opera school will never be enough! At the conservatory you might not receive enough acting, body-training or specialized musical coaching. You will have to find the right teachers with practical experience and pay for extra lessons.

## What to look for

* How many singing lessons will you get per week?
* Will you receive sufficient acting lessons?
* Are there courses in movement, dancing and fencing?
* Do they offer language courses (e. g. Italian)?
* Do the teachers have professional experience (have they worked as singers, actors and coaches in the business)?
* Are there enough school activities, such as opera productions and concerts?

## Requirements

* Your high school diploma or a graduation certificate as recognized in Germany
* A language proficiency diploma in German such as *das Große Deutsche Sprachdiplom* or *das Kleine Deutsche Sprachdiplom* of the Goethe-Institute
* To start with the first semester you should not be older than 25
* Passing an entrance examination
* Note from a qualified medical doctor

## The entrance examination

- 3 to 5 opera arias with recitative from memory in the original language (at least one in German)
- 2 German *Lieder* from memory
- Reciting from memory a spoken text in perfect German from an opera, operetta or play
- 3 piano pieces from different periods
- Be prepared to write tests in music theory and to do an aural test

The requirements vary at the different music schools. You will find the complete information on their websites.

### Applying for the entrance examination

- Fill out the application form. You can either download it from the website or apply for it in a letter or e-mail
- If you have difficulty understanding the form, contact the registrar or the International Office of the conservatory
- Usually you also have to send:
  - 2 passport photos
  - A photocopy of your passport

– A résumé (curriculum vitae, CV) in tabular form with details and certification of the contents
– Your German language diploma (certificates or diploma as notarized transcripts or photocopies)
– A list of the prepared pieces
– A prepared envelope with your address
– An international reply coupon

**Academic year**

The academic year in Germany is divided into a summer semester (from 1 April to 30 September) and a winter semester (from 1 October to 31 March). At some conservatories, you may only start your studies in the winter semester. In that case, the closing date for the admission to the entrance examination is 1 April.

**Tip**

Send your application to more than one music school. That way you will have a better chance of being accepted by at least one of them. Don't be late in sending your applications – the deadline is often very early and cannot be changed.

## Passport or visa

**Types of student visa**

If you come from a country outside the European Union you will need a visa.
However, if you are from Australia, Japan, Canada, Israel, New Zealand, USA, Switzerland, Honduras, Monaco and San Marino, you are exempted from this rule and will only need your passport.
There are three types of visas for students:
◆ A language-course visa, which cannot be subsequently converted into a student visa. This is valid only for the duration of the course.
◆ A three-month study applicant's visa, which is valid if you have not yet obtained conservatory admission. After admission, it must be converted as quickly as possible into a resident permit for student purposes at the Office for Foreign

Affairs. For this kind of visa you need proof that you have an income of at least 500 Euros per month.

* The student visa, valid for one year. In order to obtain this visa, you have to provide proof of admission and financial support for one year, at least 500 Euros per month (at time of writing).

The visa application should be submitted to the German Embassy or Consulate in your country of residence – preferably as early as possible. It can take up to 5 months before you receive the valid document.

A tourist visa cannot be converted into a student visa, and as a tourist you are not eligible for studying in Germany.

Tip

## Money makes the world go round

The cost of living is relatively high in Germany, although it varies from city to city. Cities like Berlin, Munich, Stuttgart, Frankfurt or Hamburg are more expensive than for instance Essen, Kassel, Nürnberg or Leipzig. On average you need at least 900 Euros per month for a very modest lifestyle.

If your parents cannot help you pay for your living, you should try to get a scholarship in your native country.

The German government has established a "Federal Education and Training Assistance Act" (*BAföG*). Under certain conditions, international students can apply for a *BAföG* subsidy. To find out whether you qualify for financial assistance, contact the *BAföG*-Office of the local Student Council (*das Studentenwerk*).

Tip

## Jobbing

**Work permit for students**

The good news is: foreign students may work in Germany even without a work permit. The bad news is that students who are not citizens of the European Union can work only for a limited period per year. They are allowed to work for 90 days (or 180 half-days) per year without a work permit. In some Federal States (*die Bundesländer*), they can only work during the summer vacation. The Foreign Department (*das Ausländeramt*) may authorize an additional working period of 10 hours per week with the approval of the local employment office. Students from EU countries may work without restriction.

You cannot finance a complete study course with student-jobs but you can improve your monthly income by singing. At the same time you gain useful practical experience. Learning by doing!

As a singer, you have the advantage of being a specialist. You can sing in church as a soloist, you can join an opera extra-chorus (ad-hoc chorus), work as a walk-on or super (*der Statist/die Statistin*), sing at weddings and funerals, or give singing lessons (but only if you really know what you're doing and your singing technique is perfect!).

Singing, the hard way!

## Studying possibilities

In Germany, it takes 10 semesters to do a full course in opera performance. The advantage is that you will have enough time to develop your singing skills. The great disadvantage is that if you start too late, you will be around 30 years old when you finish studying – too late to start a career! Especially for a light soprano, mezzo or lyric baritone! So think very carefully about the best time for you to start and how long you want to study. Essentially, it depends on your voice type.

* Singing is hard physical work. Breathing exercises and vocal training are a must for every day, but you have to find out for yourself how much you can practice without damaging your voice. As a beginner, you will need to be checked by your teacher, but there are exercises (especially breathing exercises) that you can do on your own (see chapter 8).

Tips

* From the first year onward, work on interpretation. A good singing technique is only the foundation for the profession. A successful opera singer must be a singing actor or actress. To be boring on stage is a deadly sin. Learn to use your imagination right from the beginning.

**Singing is imagination!**

* After a lesson you should be able to sing for another hour without feeling hoarse or having tension in your throat. Otherwise, discuss your problem with your teacher or a good coach. Be patient with yourself but do not miss the right time for a change. It is your voice and your career!

* Find out what your voice type (*das Stimmfach,* or *das Fach*) is. Do you have a light lyrical voice or a more dramatic one? Do you feel comfortable with the roles you sing? Never sing over your *Fach*! If you are having vocal difficulties, it could be that you are singing the wrong *Fach*!

> The cardinal rule for a young opera singer is: You are responsible for your own career! Nobody else can decide what is right or wrong for you. You must become master of your own fate.

* The singer of today is well informed. Take an interest in culture and politics, learn languages (especially Italian, German and French), visit the theatre and watch good movies. Be informed about new trends in the arts and literature.
* Watch good actors – half of your job will be acting!
* Acting is hard physical work. Keeping your body fit and flexible must be part of preparing to become a singer-actor.

**Keep fit**

* Strive for effortlessness. When you are on stage, nobody wants to see you work.
* It is very important to listen to CDs, watch videos and read the biographies of good singers. You will learn a lot about

their singing techniques and interpretation. But find your own way and don't copy them! No agent or opera director will give a contract to a second Fleming, Terfel or Alvarez.

## Practical experience

It is a must for singing students to gain as much practical experience as possible. That means not only singing and performing in front of an audience, but networking with people in the profession.

◆ Speak to experienced singers and ask for their advice. Do it nicely and not before an important rehearsal or opening night. You will be surprised at the feedback you get!

◆ Join the extra-chorus (ad-hoc chorus) or work as a walk-on or super. This is invaluable experience and you will get to know the assistant stage directors, coaches and singers.

◆ Work as soon as possible with an experienced musical coach. You will find them in opera houses. Usually, the bigger

the house, the better the coach. Look for their phone numbers in the Annual Theatre Directory (*das Deutsche Bühnenjahrbuch,* see www.buehnengenossenschaft.de) or leave a letter at the stage door.

* If you feel that you are not receiving enough singing lessons, try to study with your teacher privately.
* Not enough acting lessons? Look for an assistant stage director or an actor who is prepared to work with you.
* Wherever you walk, stand or sit, do it with self-confidence and be firmly convinced: I am a singer! Being tentative is one of the deadly theatre sins.

When working with an experienced musical or acting coach, beware of saying "yes-but" too often. Singing students who reach a certain level of development sometimes become "all-knowing". It is infinitely better to stay humble in the presence of a master, and to listen carefully instead of trying to prove how much you already know. Learn to shift the focus from your own ego to what is being said.

**Tip**

## Studying privately

With a few exceptions (coming from an EU country for instance), you will probably not receive a study or residence permit in order to study privately. Besides, there is the great disadvantage of being on your own. Many people are not mentally strong enough to go into the profession without the support of their family or friends and an institution like a music school. We wouldn't recommend it, unless you have a very well functioning support group and enough background knowledge to organize your life perfectly on your own.

"Anyone who goes to college to study law, medicine, or any other discipline will more or less be assured of finding a job and earning a living ... On the other hand, a voice student who gets a diploma – even one with top grades and special citations – does not have any guarantee that he'll make it. This is one of the cruel but irrefutable aspects of the singing profession ... No one should enter the singing profession thinking, 'I'm going to study voice, and my studies owe me a living'." (Placido Domingo, in: Classical Singer 1999, 7/8)

# 2 • Studying in Germany

"The self-empowerment of the singer applies to voice teaching as much as to any other aspect of career training in opera ... Singers must eventually become their own voice managers ... They may use guides to help them discover and explore their instrument, but it is the singer alone who will be out there selling the product when the curtain goes up ... Singers should take primary responsibility for their own education and for their own discovery of the knowledge that will aid them in creating believable performances." (Helfgot/Beeman, The Third Line)

# 3

# Auditioning

## Introduction

At the time of writing, there were approximately 90 music theatres in the German-speaking countries. Most of them have a *festes Ensemble*. Being *fest* in an opera house means that you have a permanent position with a monthly salary and the social security that comes with it. Germany, Austria and Switzerland are the only countries in the world that offer this possibility. There are 12 opera houses in Austria and 6 German-speaking opera houses in Switzerland. It is thus easy to understand why Germany is the country to which young singers flock from all over the world like hummingbirds around a flower.

In the 2004/2005 season, in Germany alone, 2,976 opera singers were in permanent or guest positions as soloists. Considering the fact that 4,000 to 6,000 singers from all over the world come to Germany annually in order to audition for these positions, and considering the fact that in every given year there are probably only at the most 50 new vacancies in all voice categories, the chances of finding a job are very small. If you're not very talented and extremely well prepared, there's very little chance of finding a singing job in Germany.

## The opera season

The opera season (*die Spielzeit*) in most German houses goes from mid-August to end of June of the subsequent year. Some will go from the middle of September to the end of July. All opera houses close for six weeks during the European summer. This is the time where you may either have a well-earned holiday or sing in one of the many summer festivals.

# 3 ◆ Auditioning

## Repertoire

**Be versatile**

During the season, an opera house offers five to six opera performances a week. In a single season, a house might add four to five new operas to their existing repertoire. Some houses renew their repertoire regularly, getting rid of their old productions fairly quickly, while others (mainly the bigger) houses often repeat existing productions for many years, adding new operas all the time. In practical terms, this means that the *fest* singers are always learning new parts and adding to their personal repertoire. But it also means that a singer applying for a vacancy has to be very versatile and must fit into the needs of the house. You may find that you will have to sing roles under or over your *Fach* (voice type). If you feel that you should only specialize in such roles as Norma or La Sonnambula and it is beneath you to sing a "run-of-the-mill" Susanna or Despina then you might just find yourself exclusively entertaining your private circle of friends with your very special qualities. The German opera houses will not be able to fit you into their plans.

## When to audition

For the singer coming from outside, it is useful to know that the main time to audition in the opera houses is October/November and sometimes February/March because this is the time when the houses start looking for new talent for the next season, which starts after the summer break. The agents will start hearing singers in August/September. Because there are so many singers looking for jobs, the agents have waiting lists. It is therefore a very good idea to apply for an audition long before the time. As most agents close down their offices for the summer break, this means

When you audition for a vacancy as an opera singer, it is essential that you think of yourself as a product that you want to sell. The same rules of supply and demand that apply to other businesses are also valid for this profession. There is the intermediary (the agent), who has to recommend the best product (the singer) to the buyer (the opera director).

that you have to start applying in June for an audition in September for a job starting in August of the following year! This sounds crazy but that's the way it works. Obviously there are exceptions to this rule and there have been cases where singers have auditioned and have been taken immediately or an opera house might hold auditions very late in the season. They can afford to wait because the market is "overflowing".

## General requirements

### Language skills

* It is not enough to have a basic knowledge of German. **German** Nowadays agents will refuse to listen to you if you do not speak German well enough for everyday negotiations and for the opera stage. A lot of German operas require dialogue (e. g. in *Der Freischütz* or *Die Zauberflöte*). As you will be living and working in Germany, it goes without saying that you have to be in total command of the language.

* Of course Italian is still the opera language *numero uno*. It **Italian** is important to speak Italian. It is not good enough to know the pronunciation of the opera text. Imagine trying to make a Mozart or Rossini recitative sound natural and interesting if you do not know the first thing about the rhythms and melody of the spoken language! Imagine having to take over a role in Italian at short notice and not knowing what the other singers are saying! Especially in operas with recitatives, this can be very embarrassing. We recommend a language course in Italy. The best way to learn Italian is to live with an Italian family and take an intensive course of at least four weeks (see appendix: websites).

* As the middle and bigger houses increasingly present the **French and other** French, Czech and Russian operas in the original languages, **languages** we recommend that you learn at least the rules of pronunciation in these languages.

# 3 • Auditioning

**Singing skills**

Your singing ability should be sufficiently advanced so that you will not need to concentrate on your singing technique, but are free to interpret your roles.

**Acting skills**

This means that you will be expected to convince and hold your audience. It is definitely not good enough to arrive with a few arias and think that this will get you a job. If you do not have the possibility of preparing your roles in a good opera school, at least do an acting course with a skilled professional and study with a good musical coach who will not only correct your musical mistakes but help you find the meaning behind the notes as well. The agent will only be interested in someone with personality and imagination.

**Body skills**

You have to be physically very fit, not only for travelling and the general stress, but also for the stage work itself (see chapter 7).

It is important to be physically so flexible that you are able to use your body as an instrument on stage. A singer who cannot do this is at a distinct disadvantage.

You should also take lessons in dancing. Remember that you will be expected to waltz on stage (e.g. in *La Traviata* or operetta in general), do the fandango (*Le nozze di Figaro*) or do American jazz dancing (i.e. *West Side Story*).

**Overweight**

It is important not to be overweight. Not only is this bad for your general health but the opera managers today refuse to cast overweight singers unless they have an exceptional singing and acting ability. Even world-class singers are being dropped today because of being overweight.

Learn to look after yourself from the beginning. Take the responsibility for your career in your own hands.

## Discipline and responsibility

One of the most important requirements for a successful career is discipline. When you arrive in Germany, you are on your own. No singing teacher or agent is going to hold your hand and tell you when to work on your voice, how to learn your roles and how to organise your everyday life.

Do not blindly accept everything your singing teacher, your family or your friends might have told you. Go and find out for yourself where you stand and what you need!

The first thing to do is talk to a professional (not only a singing teacher but maybe a stage director, conductor or a singer who has sufficient experience in the business) and find out whether your dream of becoming a singer is realistic. If you know of somebody who is already working in Germany, you should write and ask them for advice.

**Talk to professionals**

This also means taking responsibility for your finances. A lot of our readers come from countries where it is very difficult to find sponsors or financial support from families or other sources. You could clean people's houses or do babysitting. Once you are in Germany it will help if you have some other skill or qualification apart from singing. A friend of ours learnt how to do shiatsu massage and managed to finance her singing studies at home and later in Germany in this way. Computer or typing skills can also be of great value. Of course, you should not spend too much time acquiring a non-singing skill because you would then waste valuable time. The sooner you concentrate on a singing career the better. Otherwise you may arrive in Germany and find out that you have missed the boat because you are by now too old to start your career.

**Finances**

## Knowledge and self-knowledge

It is very important that you learn to observe yourself absolutely objectively. Make video or sound recordings of your lessons and performances and learn to listen and look at yourself critically and objectively.

Read the biographies of famous opera singers. Listen to recordings of good singers and conductors. Go to the opera

Look at yourself objectively

**35**

regularly or watch as many opera videos as possible. Learn to be observant. Find out what the profession is all about! Compare your abilities to those of the professionals. Become your own best critic.

**Business sense**

Being fully prepared also means that you have to develop business sense. Learn to sell yourself! We have known at least four potentially world-class singers (with great voices and acting ability) who have failed in the profession because they were absolutely clueless about "the singing business" (see chapter 6).

**Behaviour in a foreign country**

Being fully prepared also means that you must know how to behave in a foreign country. Every country has different rules of conduct (see chapters 1 and 6).

## Ambition

There are singers who have known that they wanted to be opera singers for as long as they can remember. Then there are those who are not quite so sure whether they really want to sing. These singers usually have many other interests and hobbies which satisfy them as much as singing and they would probably be quite as happy in another profession. They are at an enormous disadvantage in the opera market.

If you do not have the conviction or the "inner flame" which burns brightly and tells you that there is nothing else on earth that can satisfy you as much as singing on the opera stage, you will never make it in this business.

It is not enough to have a beautiful voice. What is essential is the ambition and single-mindedness behind the voice. Then again there are many singers burning with ambition and dying to be opera singers, who simply don't have enough talent. It is difficult for such singers to know why they are not getting anywhere despite their intense wish to be on stage. We advise every young singer to be as realistic as possible and to develop sensitivity for the feedback they are getting. Analyze very carefully who praises you and who criticizes

you. Give yourself enough time but don't wait so long that it will be too late to start another profession.

If you are as prepared as you can be and you still find that after two or three years of auditioning you have no success in finding a job, you should stop blaming the agents and opera managers and start analyzing your own talent. Are the people who praise you professionals in the business or are they perhaps only well-meaning friends who love you and want to make you feel good? Are you getting consistent negative feedback from agents? This process can be very painful, but it is important to be objective about yourself and not to wait too long before making a decision about your future.

**No success in finding a job?**

## What to aim for

If you have a non-European passport, you should try for a permanent (*fest*) position.
The advantages are:

+ You receive a contract for a certain number of years
+ You receive a monthly salary with social security and unemployment benefits
+ You have the opportunity to develop your roles in familiar and secure surroundings
+ You automatically receive a German work and residence permit

**Tip**

If you happen to be married and/or have children, you should make sure that this step is the right one for everyone. Does your partner support you in your decisions? Is he or she prepared to accompany you to Germany? Could your partner find work there? How will your family cope with the new language and cultural differences?

## Finding your "Fach"

+ Ask the advice of not only your singing teacher, but other experienced professionals working in the theatre. Do they think that your voice is suitable for the roles you are learning?
+ Are you the right physical type for the *Fach* you want to sing? A tenor who wants to audition as Tamino but looks more like a Pedrillo should reconsider the package he wants to present to an agent.
+ What is the intrinsic quality of your voice? Do you have the "Schmalz" for the Italian repertoire or is your voice more suitable for the German repertoire?
+ You could go to a voice clinic and have your vocal folds (also called vocal chords) measured. This will give you an indication of your voice range but you should not solely rely on this.

**Tip**

Don't sing the heavier roles too soon!
Most of the young singers who come to Germany to find a singing job are singing over their *Fach*! You may think that

you are a Butterfly or a Calaf because it feels so wonderful to sing and it sounds so marvellous (to you!), but without many years of experience, you should not attempt the big *Fach* too soon. Only a very small section of the singing population is born with a huge voice ready to tackle a Siegfried or Turandot. The rest of us have to start off singing the more lyrical parts, even if the voice may one day potentially grow and develop into a dramatic tenor or soprano. Apart from this, if you have had no stage experience (and that also means no acting experience), there is no way in the world that you will be able to sing and act a complex and highly emotional part like, for instance, Butterfly. You will have no time to think about acting or singing technique but will have to concentrate every bit of your artistic and emotional energy on creating a believable person on stage.

Experience means knowing how to look at the conductor from the corner of your eye, without the audience noticing it. Experience means solving vocal problems automatically without thinking about breath support or voice placement. Experience means having the vocal and physical stamina to get through a strenuous role. Experience means fitting into an ensemble both musically and dramatically. Experience means knowing what to do when something goes wrong onstage. Experience means knowing which acting technique to use when a director wants a certain effect. And, last but not least, experience means controlling your emotions onstage and not getting overwhelmed by them.

*What is experience?*

## Choosing your repertoire

Once you feel technically secure you should acquire a sufficiently large repertoire within your voice type (*das Stimmfach* or *das Fach*). Do not come to Germany without knowing at least 5 or 6 roles. You are not auditioning as a singer of arias. You are auditioning for a role.

*Your audition repertoire*

# 3 ◆ Auditioning

◆ One of your five operatic audition roles should be in German, one in Italian and one in French. You should present at least one Mozart role. Be prepared that most of the opera houses in Germany perform their operas in the original language. You might even be expected to sing the Russian operas in the original. The exception being the French operettas and the opera *Die Verkaufte Braut* (The Bartered Bride), which are usually done in German.

◆ It is very important to have at least two operetta roles in your repertoire.

◆ The roles should be chosen from the repertoire that is currently being performed in Germany. Read the opera magazines to find out which roles are in demand (don't forget operetta and the musicals). There is no point in auditioning with an aria from *I Puritani* or *Fedora* if the opera houses never perform these operas.

◆ Do not sing lieder or arias from oratorio.

◆ Always learn the recitative that belongs to the aria.

◆ If possible – specialize! If you happen to be a lyric mezzo, you will soon discover that you are one of 200 other mezzos all auditioning with Cherubino and Dorabella, so you should try and find additional roles which are more specialized or more difficult. If you have a good coloratura technique you should learn the bravura Rossini or Handel arias instead of being the 200th Cherubino. It goes without saying that you will also need to have Cherubino and Dorabella in your standard repertoire, even if you sing more showy arias. A tenor with a good high C should choose arias with wonderful top notes. Many opera houses in Germany perform operetta and musicals. If you have a good song from a musical, you could add this to your repertoire. If you know a brilliant dance routine, so much the better! But remember that the musicals often are performed in German and you will be expected to speak dialogues perfectly. You should also have a monologue ready in German.

◆ Apart from the five or six roles that you are preparing for your audition tour, you should at least look at all the roles of your repertoire. An agent might ask you if you know a specific role and it can only be in your favour if you can answer that you have looked at the part but for instance feel that the second aria is not quite ready. Or that you have looked at the part and should be able to learn it in a few days. Don't however try to sight-read it at the audition. If the agent is interested you will be given time to learn it.

♦ If you want to sing a particularly long aria for example an aria with five verses or Zerbinetta's aria, which takes 12 minutes to sing, then you should ask your coach to work out some sensible cuts for you (but without cutting out the difficult bits). This will be very welcome as nobody wants to sit through reams of music.

**Your friend the role**

It is extremely difficult to go out onto a naked stage and sell yourself as an opera singer without make-up, costumes, props, colleagues and orchestra. If you go out there only as yourself, you have already lost half the battle. Your only friend will be the role you are singing. If you can use your imagination to stay inside the character and portray it only with your thoughts, eyes and a few gestures, then you have won half the battle. Before you audition, your arias should be prepared as completely as possible, musically, vocally, linguistically and most important of all, dramatically.

"To stand and sing an aria for an audition is more challenging visually and theatrically than to perform a role with costumes and props. Yet singers can sell their talents during a single 'stand and sing' audition. Singers with highly developed expressive abilities will stand apart from the other auditionees – this could well be the making of their career" (Helfgot/Beeman, The Third Line).

## Preparing for auditions

♦ Discuss with your singing teacher which roles you should be learning. Then study these roles until they are technically perfect.
♦ Do not only learn roles that you love to sing. See to it that you cover the whole repertoire that will be expected of you (see appendix: audition arias).

# 3 • Auditioning

**What is a good coach?**

When you have learnt the notes and solved the technical difficulties, study with a good musical coach. Good coaches look at every detail and do not allow mistakes. They not only listen to the notes but advise on musicality, style and phrasing. They know how important the words are and emphasize diction and interpretation. They have excellent hearing and can therefore help with vocal problems. They speak the opera languages (German, Italian and French) perfectly. Some coaches also specialize in Slavic languages. They will know the repertoire and can help you choose the roles you should be learning. They can also give valuable tips on what will be expected of you during an audition. If you live in a country where there are no good coaches, you should at least try to find out who the best available one is, even if it entails travelling.

**Why the acting teacher?**

Study the arias with an acting teacher. Ideally, you should have sung the role on stage. As this is not always possible, the next best thing is to find an expert who can show you how to present the aria credibly. You can also do much on your own. Look at the whole role first and analyze the character you are singing. Then analyze the aria you have chosen word for word. Write down the meaning and the feeling of each word. Then decide on the emotional content. What is the overall intent of the aria – what emotions do you want to convey?

It goes without saying that you should know exactly what every word of the aria means – never work with a general translation.

Act through the aria. Imagine the character and the space around it. Are you in a garden? Are you alone? Is it a monologue or are you addressing someone? Then speak the aria without the music as if you were an actor. Infuse every word with the appropriate meaning. The next step would be to use a few props and movements. Act out the aria as if you were onstage. You may jump on chairs or stand completely still as long as you are giving a valid interpretation of the character. Use movements, gestures and facial expressions. Practice in front of the mirror. Learn to use your eyes! This is only possible if you know how to use the so-called subtext or inner script (see chapter 9). This means that

42

you must be thinking what the character is thinking. Never stop being the character! That also means that you have to give meaning to the musical interludes. Many singers don't know what to do during musical introductions and connecting passages and feel embarrassed and

> Never present an audition aria without preparing the dramatic content just as thoroughly as the singing aspect.

awkward when they are not singing. This is where the subtext is particularly handy. During a long interlude, you should have a ready-made script in your mind. Only after you have done all this work will it be possible to audition the aria. You will then find that you no longer need the props or movements because you will be using your imagination, and therefore have no difficulty staying within the character and telling the story even when standing still.

◆ Listen to different recordings of your arias to learn the correct style and interpretation, but do not copy the singer. Preserve your individuality.

◆ Learn how to walk onto the stage and how to announce yourself. This has to be practised just as much as everything else. Find out how to do this in German and practise it until you are perfect. Remember that the first impression is lasting, even before you open your mouth.

## Finding a job

There are two ways of going about finding a job. You could sing for one of the many agents in Germany, Switzerland and Austria, or you could contact the opera houses directly. We recommend the first method unless you are well versed in negotiating your own contracts in a foreign language. Some opera houses actually prefer to use agents as intermediaries because otherwise they might have to plough through an enormous amount of bad singers before finding the jewels. Other houses prefer not to use agents. If you have enough confidence to sell yourself to an opera house without an agent, you should call the managing office (*das künstlerische*

Auditioning for an agent or opera house?

*Betriebsbüro,* abbr. *KBB)* of the house for an appointment. You will find the addresses on the Internet or in the official opera directory (*das Deutsche Bühnenjahrbuch*). This can be ordered at www.buehnengenossenschaft.de under *Publikationen.* Even if they do not have a vacancy, you could ask to sing anyway, just to be on their books. This is called *das Vorsingen zur Information.*

## Auditioning for agents

The addresses of the agents can also be found in the *Deutsches Bühnenjahrbuch.* Once you have sung for an agent, he or she will send you to the individual opera houses. Be prepared to travel. The whole auditioning process can take a few months. Plan on staying at least three months and buy a Eurail ticket before you come over.

Tip

You will have to come on a tourist visa, which is only valid for three months. Therefore you should plan your stay carefully to fit in as many dates as possible. Organize your finances beforehand. You will need at least 2,500 Euros for three months including accommodation, travelling and food. The cheapest accommodation especially in big cities is the youth hostel (*die Jugendherberge*). A bed and breakfast will cost about 22 Euros per night. Go to your local youth hostel beforehand and ask for a "Hostelling International Card". For further information, look up the website www.jugendherberge.de.

Categories of
agencies

There are three categories of agencies in Germany, Switzerland and Austria:
* The three or four top agencies that have the stars on their books. They are not interested in beginners.
* The middle-sized agencies that have been in the business a long time.
* The small agencies with two or three employees. They are often highly motivated to help young artists.

You should try to sing for as many agents as possible in the last two categories.

There are also some very good agents in France, Spain and Italy, but for the beginning, we recommend staying in the German-speaking countries.

As a young singer starting off in Germany, you are under no obligation to sign an exclusive contract with one agent. It is better to sing for many agents until you have found the one who loves your voice and is prepared to get you work. If you find yourself in the situation where an agent wants to send you to sing at a certain opera house, but another agent has already mentioned this house, it is not ethical to accept the second offer. You should ask the first agent to arrange the audition date. Above all, be honest and tell your agent the truth. Once you feel that you have found an agent who seems to be working actively for you, it is a good idea to stay exclusively with him. If he knows that you are loyal to him, he will also be loyal to you.

**Exclusive contract?**

* If you have the chance to talk to a soloist working in a German opera house, then do not hesitate to ask his or her advice.
* Once you have sung for an agent, ask for his advice and then weigh the answers according to your own instincts. Even if he criticizes, the tips and recommendations he gives might prove to be very useful.

**Tips**

After an audition you will very often hear "thank you" without any further comment. This is the typical "don't call us, we'll call you" situation and means that the agent is not interested in what you have to offer.

Try to find out which specific houses an agent works with and which other singers they have placed in jobs. Some agents boast about what they can do for you, but do not necessarily have enough clout with the important opera houses to get you the job.

**Don't call us, we'll call you**

**45**

# 3 ◆ Auditioning

**Agent fee**

If an agent gets you a job, the fee can be up to 12% of your monthly salary for one entire year (meaning one opera season). This is negotiable. Some opera houses will pay 50% of the agent's fee, so you have only to pay the other 50%. Other houses, depending on their structure, will not do this, which means that you will then have to pay the full amount yourself. In this case, try to negotiate with your agent.

For concert work, an agent is allowed to ask up to 15% of your fee. This is also negotiable.

## The ZBF

### Where to start

The *Zentrale Bühnen-, Fernseh- und Filmvermittlung* (abbr. ZBF) is a state-owned agency and does not charge a fee. This is a good place to start your audition tour. They have branches in Cologne, Berlin, Hamburg, Munich and Leipzig.

**Tip**

An agent is not a manager and will not work exclusively for you. He or she might also represent other singers singing your *Fach*.

After you have sent in your application to an agent, you might not get an answer immediately. Should this be the case, wait for a few weeks and then call and ask if your letter has arrived. If it has, ask for an audition date. You might get the answer "sorry we're full up". Don't be discouraged. Ask when and where the next auditions will be held and then call again the day before the auditions. Very often, there are short-notice cancellations.

**What can the agent do for you?**

He or she will
* give you general advice on managing your career
* give you advice about your *Fach*
* set up auditions with opera houses
* get you concert work
* follow your artistic development and come to your performances
* negotiate the fee

# The application

You have to prepare
* a cover letter (*der Begleitbrief*)
* your photo (*das Foto*)
* your résumé (curriculum vitae, CV) (*der Lebenslauf*)
* a list of your repertoire (*die Repertoireliste*)
* a CD or tape of at least three opera arias (no lieder or oratorio). This should only be sent if the agent requires it, but you must have one ready

See appendix for examples of cover letter, CV and repertoire list.

An agent gets an enormous amount of applications per day. Therefore, yours should not be more than three of four pages at the most. Just give the most important information.

**Tip**

The letter should be as short as possible and should contain only the following information:
* your address and telephone numbers where you can be reached in Europe
* your voice type
* the kind of position for which you want to sing (soloist, studio or chorus)
* in which season you want to start

**The cover letter**

Your photo should not be bigger than 9×13 centimetres (4×6 inches). It may be in colour, but a black-and-white photo is absolutely fine.
Do not send more than one photo. It should be taken by a professional photographer who knows how to show you at your best and it should be a head-and-shoulder shot, preferably taken in a studio with a neutral background. Do not send photos of yourself in costume. The photo need not be over-glamorous but should show your sparkling personality. Looking straight into the camera will show your eyes and

**The photo**

# 3 ◆ Auditioning

personality to your best advantage. Don't send private photos of yourself on the beach or standing against a tree in the woods – this is considered extremely unprofessional. You may either send a glossy (remember to put your name and address on the back), or you may scan it into your computer and print it onto your résumé or CV (see Appendix). This is cheaper in the long run, as you will not get your glossies back from the agent. If you scan, don't forget to print the photo in optimal quality. It will not be good enough if you just copy it.

**The photo is extremely important because it gives a first impression.**

**Tip**

Some agents accept applications via e-mail, but we find it more professional to send it by conventional mail unless the agent specifically asks for e-mail. Be careful of sending big files via e-mail. We once received a 10 megabyte file from a young singer because she did not know that the photo had not been converted into a convenient e-mail size!

**Your résumé**

The first page should contain your
* name, address and telephone numbers where you can be reached in Europe
* date of birth (it is unprofessional to lie about your age)
* voice type
* your scanned photo

The second page should list, in tabular form,
* a summary of your school qualifications
* a list of your artistic qualifications (including where, when and what you studied),
* the languages you speak
* master classes you have taken
* competitions or prizes you have won
* your sung repertoire. These are the roles that you have performed on the opera stage. You can do this in tabular form, specifying the work, the composer and the role. Also *where* and *when* you have sung it. You can mention school performances in which you have sung the big roles of your

*Fach*. Do not mention small roles or roles that are not part of your present *Fach*. This means that if you are selling yourself as a Figaro, you do not necessarily want to mention that you have done Antonio at your music school unless you have not performed much and need the roles for your repertoire list.

* learnt repertoire. These are the roles that you have learnt musically because they belong to your *Fach*, but have not performed on stage yet.
* a list of the arias with which you intend to audition

**Tip**

In Germany, one starts the CV with the older date and ends with the most recent.

Do not give superfluous details like names of parents, religion, hobbies or a long list of all your teachers (unless they are internationally recognized).

Do not mention every private or house concert in which you have ever sung. The agents are only interested in full performances you have sung with orchestra.

Under no circumstances should you include actual certificates, qualifications, awards, programs of your performances or photocopies of newspaper reviews. If you happen to have good reviews, then photocopy the sentences concerning your achievement with the name of the newspaper and the date it appeared, the opera and the venue. Thus, all your reviews will fit onto one page and the agents do not have to read through reams of unnecessary text. You can be sure that they will not do this. They will throw everything into the wastepaper basket with glee!

Your repertoire list should contain arias from opera, operetta and musical. If you have sung a lot of oratorio or lieder this should be mentioned in one sentence without going into detail.

The roles and operas should be written in the original language. It is important not to make spelling mistakes. This makes a very bad impression.

**49**

Do not write about yourself in the third person. This is appropriate for press releases but not for a job application.

Your application should be written on a computer. Do not write by hand and do not use coloured paper. It is unnecessary to put the papers into a file or to make an art work out of them. The simpler and more business-like it is, the better impression you will make. Just send the loose sheets in a big envelope. Don't forget to put your name and address on each sheet.

Should the agent ask for a recording, it goes without saying that this should be professionally done. You should invest in a good pianist and have the recording done by an expert, in a proper sound studio (*das Tonstudio*). Do not record more than three opera arias, but choose the arias that show your voice at its best.

## Preparing for your audition tour

◆ Before you travel to Germany you should read as much as you can about the country. Buy a good travel guide and come prepared.

◆ Find out if you can use your mobile phone in Germany. If not, be prepared to buy a cheap cell phone (*das Handy*) with a pay-as-you-go card in Germany.

◆ Book an inexpensive hotel for a few weeks as a first base. This is quite easy through the Internet. From there, you should try to find an inexpensive furnished apartment or room, because this will be far cheaper in the long run (see chapter 1). If you are travelling and you find yourself without a place to stay, go to the main station and ask at the Tourist Information counter for a cheap hotel.

◆ If you are taking important medication, see to it that you pack them. You might not find the same ones in Germany.

◆ Remember that it could be winter in Germany when you arrive. Pack enough warm clothing. Don't forget your umbrella and waterproof shoes.

- Travel light. Don't bring the kitchen sink! See to it that you have comfortable travelling clothes and one good outfit (with the right shoes) for auditioning. Remember, you can wash your underclothes in hotel rooms and go to local laundries. There is nothing wrong with wearing the same clothes every second day. You are not on a fashion tour. After the first few weeks of travelling and "schlepping", you will be very grateful for this advice.
- We recommend travelling by train. Get a Eurail Pass before you leave.
- You do not have to bring theatre make-up. If you are lucky enough to get a chance to perform, the make-up will be provided by the theatre.

## Preparing for your first audition

- Make a copy of your list of audition arias to give to the agent in case the one you sent is for some reason not available.
- Prepare your sheet music so that the pianist will have no difficulty reading it. You can paste photocopies of your arias into a spiral ring book or you could mark the arias in your score in such a way that they can be found immediately. It should be easy to turn the pages in the score as well as in the spiral ring book! Cuts or specific tempo requirements must be clearly marked in order to avoid disagreeable surprises.
- Remember to pack your throat lozenges, some painkillers (but not aspirin, see chapter 7), a bottle of water, an apple or banana and anything else that you might need. If you have to travel far, you might want to take a sandwich. Some singers might want to take a warm sweater for the long wait. Others might need a good book as a distraction.
- See to it that you warm up your voice thoroughly beforehand. Once you arrive, there may not be a room available. We have known singers who have had to warm up their voices in the parking lot! You might want to pack a portable keyboard.
- Do not travel far on the day of the audition. If possible, you should arrive | Never arrive late for an audition!

**51**

# 3 ♦ Auditioning

the day before, so that you are rested when you have to sing. Travelling by train is less stressful than by car.

♦ Prepare yourself mentally for the fact that there could be thirty or more singers auditioning on one day. You may have to wait hours before getting to sing.

♦ Teach yourself the humming exercises (see chapter 8) that can be done without disturbing the others, so that you can warm up your voice again if necessary.

## The first impression

When you audition, your first impression is made from the moment you walk onto the stage.
This can be influenced by

♦ your clothing
♦ the way you make your entrance
♦ how your personality comes across

If any of these is unsuitable, you may already have lost even before singing the first note! If two singers are equally good, the singer who makes the best first impression might just get the job. Put your audition clothes on and practise walking in them at home in front of the mirror or ask a good friend to observe you objectively and critically. Never underestimate the effect of a charming smile and a bounce in your step!

### Your audition wardrobe
The student look is out. You should dress like a professional. That does not mean that you have to exaggerate and wear white scarves like Pavarotti or drape yourself with jewels like Caballé – they've made it, they may do it. We suggest the elegant understatement.

**Women**

Women should wear a dress or a smart blouse with a skirt. No slacks, unless you are auditioning exclusively for trouser parts (*die Hosenrolle*) like Cherubino or Oktavian. Wear the colours that suit you. You might have a gorgeous emerald-green dress in your closet that shows off your hair or eye colour! It is important to show yourself at your best. If you have not quite reached your ideal weight, you might want to wear something more loose fitting that does not accentuate every curve. Ladies, please, evening and cocktail dresses are not appropriate! Your dress or skirt should be short enough to show your nice legs. We suggest a length

> Avoid wearing only black or dark brown. It will make you disappear into a dark background.

just under the knee, not shorter – remember that you might be singing onstage and the listeners will be looking up at you! Your shoes should be elegant and have a slight heel. Flat shoes are unflattering. Boots are out. Your hair should be out of your face – a big fringe is counterproductive because nobody will be able to see your facial expression. Don't wear too much jewellery – especially if it gets in your way or makes tinkling noises! Loose chiffon scarves that tend to come undone while you are singing can also be very distracting.

**Men**

For the men, we suggest a blazer, a pair of slacks, and an open-necked shirt or a roll neck (turtleneck). If you have a stunning tie, wear it! You could wear a suit and tie if it makes you feel good but this is not obligatory. Never wear sneakers – this is "verboten"! A good pair of leather shoes or loafers will make a far better impression.

If you have difficulty in deciding what to wear, we suggest that you invest in a consultation with a fashion stylist. Not only women but also men can benefit hugely from finding out what style and colour suits them.

## The audition

Sometimes when you audition for agents they might ask for a list of your audition arias, which you should have with you. Everything else – coat, scarf, gloves, big or small bag – should be left behind. Do not take your water bottle or even a glass of water with you. This makes a bad impression. When you sing a role on stage, you also can't take your water with you! Walk on with a spring in your step and a smile on your face. Remember to look at the audience while coming in. If your accompanist does not yet have your music, then go to him from behind the piano, because you do not necessarily want to show your backside to the audience, and give him your music. Stay calm and take your time. You might want to point out a certain cut or tempo change in case you have not had a chance to rehearse with him. Then walk confidently to your position – central stage but not so far from the pianist, that you can't hear him or her. Introduce yourself in German with a firm, clear, projected voice. You will then be asked which aria you want to sing. You then announce the aria (*die Arie*) in German, but using the original language for the title. You do not have to say *"Ich singe die Arie 'Non so più, cosa son cosa faccio' aus Le nozze di Figaro von Wolfgang Amadeus Mozart"*. It suffices to say *"ich singe die erste Cherubino-Arie"*. Only if the aria is not very well known should you give the full title. It is also not necessary to give the composers' first names unless there are two with the same surname.

Under no circumstances should you give excuses like "I am a bit tired", or "I have a cold" or "it was very dry on the plane". Just go in there and get on with the job – nobody wants to hear excuses.

When you feel ready to sing, give the accompanist a slight nod. Once he starts playing, you might discover that the tempo is different from the one you are used to. This could mean two things. Either the pianist is excellent and knows the ideal tempo of this specific aria, or he doesn't have a clue, and is heading you towards a disaster. It would be a mistake to start waving your arms around, or stamping your feet to show him your tempo. You should stop singing and ask for a short break in order to discuss the tempo with the pianist. On the other hand, you might feel technically confident enough to sing the aria in the tempo he is suggesting. Then do this without

> When you walk on, you should only have the essentials with you: your sheet music and your sparkling personality.

> You should practise your announcement in front of the mirror or with a teacher, so that there are no glitches.

showing any irritation. If you can't hear the piano clearly at the place where you stand, ask for a short break, giving the reason and put yourself quickly into a better position. Do all these necessary changes without any fuss!

Sometimes there are too many singers auditioning and you might be asked to sing only one aria. Choose the one that

> Never try out an aria that you do not know well enough. This is only permissible if you have been asked to learn an aria for a specific job. Otherwise, you should be able to sing your arias in your sleep!

shows your technical and musical abilities at their best. Don't choose the easiest one! If the aria you want to sing is very long (e. g. Zerbinetta) or has five stanzas, then you should work out a sensible version (with a few cuts) beforehand. But don't eliminate the difficult bits – that's what the agent wants to hear.

When singing for agents, you will probably not have a chance to rehearse with the pianist. You should be prepared for this. In some cases, you might have to pay the pianist a small fee. It is not common to bring your own pianist to an audition. You may do this if you want to, but he/she might have to wait around for hours. This could become expensive.

**Tip**

Never sing if you are ill, unless it is just a slight cold and you feel that your voice will still show its optimal quality. In every other case – bad headache, bronchitis, laryngitis or anything that will hinder you from giving your best – cancel, rather than trying to sing. If you sing badly, the agent will make a note of it and will always remember you negatively. Don't leave "cookies"! Rather ask for a later audition date. It is our experience that young singers do not take this rule very seriously. But trust us! It will count against you if you do not sing well because of bad cold or any other mishap!

**A case in point**

A student of ours suffered a slipped disc in the train on the way to a very important audition. She felt she could not cancel at such a short notice, and sang even though she was in extreme pain. She never heard from them again, although she was good enough to get the part.

## Auditioning in an opera house

Once the agent has chosen you, he will send you to the different opera houses that may be looking for your voice type. He will let you know the time and place. If the agent tells you to sing a specific aria there is usually a good reason. It is nevertheless a good idea to call the opera house beforehand and ask exactly what voice type they are looking for just to make sure. Misunderstandings have been known to happen.

The same general audition rules for agents also apply to auditions in opera houses, except that there is a better chance that you will get to rehearse with the pianist. This means that it is always a good idea to arrive an hour before the audition time.

If you call the opera house directly without an agent, ask for the artistic office (*das Betriebsbüro*) and find out what they are planning for the next season. If they are planning *Il Barbiere di Siviglia*, then sing the Figaro aria instead of the Billy Budd aria you were planning to sing. The golden rule is: sing what they want to hear! You could also look on the Internet to find out what operas are being done in this specific house.

You will probably be singing on the main stage and the opera director (*der Intendant/die Intendantin*) and other members of the artistic staff will be sitting in the auditorium. Do not be put off if they talk amongst themselves or do not seem to be interested. This should not influence your performance.

When you have finished your first aria, they might ask you to sing a second, and offer you a break. They might then hear another singer while you prepare yourself mentally for your next aria. If there are no other singers then you must be prepared to sing your second aria immediately. Usually the first aria will be of your own choice and should be the aria that shows all your abilities at their best. The second aria will be chosen by the house. If they say "thank you very much" after the first aria, this could mean that they are not interested. You should try to ask them after the audition for an opinion. You will then either hear "we have nothing to say at the moment" or "we have to hear some more singers", which mostly means they are not interested. Or they will call you into the office and offer you a contract. If they give you specific advice even without an offer, this may count as a success for you!

A friend of ours was told by a very big house to work on certain faults and come back after a year. She did this and then got the job.

**A case in point**

If you are offered a contract, you should hear what they have to say and then ask for a day or two to think it over or discuss it with your agent. This is standard procedure and does not mean that you are jeopardizing your chances. Unless you are very confident and know exactly what the house normally pays its singers, it is always better to discuss the offer with someone knowledgeable about the business. This should be your agent or a trusted, informed colleague. But you will find that a beginner's contract leaves little room for negotiation. You will be offered a certain salary; a certain length of time (usually one or at the most two years) and you will be informed which roles you will be singing. The only negotiable point will be the roles. If you feel that you might not be able to sing the offered roles in one season, either because there are too many to learn or one of them is not really in your *Fach*, then you could try to negotiate this. But remember that there are other singers out there who are prepared to sing everything they are offered – even if it means ruining their voices. Some houses are unscrupulous and would rather take that option than have endless discussions with a "difficult" singer. This is where you have to be mentally strong and weigh your possibilities. If you honestly feel that the house will be exploiting you and that your voice would not stand the strain, it will be better not to accept the contract.

**The contract**

The basic rules of good conduct and courteousness also count in the opera world. You should be humble, but not subservient, confident, but not abrasive.

**Tip**

# 3 ♦ Auditioning

## Studios

Trainee programs Some opera houses in Germany have a young singer's program, mostly called a studio (*das Opernstudio*). This changes from year to year but it might be worth your while to ask the agents about this option. It offers you the opportunity to develop artistically during the period between music school and full professional activity. You become a member of the house ensemble, singing small roles for a small salary, while still learning from the coaches and stage directors. There is usually an age limit.

## Competitions and Master Classes

When you start looking for a job, it could be advantageous to take part in some of the bigger European singing competitions. This will help you practice the audition process and give you an idea of your present stage of development. Find out which competitions are attended by the opera *Intendanten* (e. g. the Belvedere in Vienna, the Bertelsmann in Gütersloh or The Singer of the World Competition in Cardiff).

It is important to select the appropriate competitions and not to spend too much valuable time on too many competitions in general. We have known singers who have become addicted to them and travel from one competition to the next for years on end without ever starting a singing career.

You should also take part in master classes by great singers, because this will assist your networking and could help you get a foot in the door. You will find information on competitions and workshops in the opera magazines and the Internet.

## Extra jobs

While looking for a job, it might be a good idea to work as a super or walk-on (*der Statist/die Statistin*) in one of the big opera houses. You could also audition for the ad hoc chorus (*der Extrachor*). This will give you the experience of working in an opera house and the possibility of making valuable contacts.

Do not be discouraged if you are not successful during your first few auditions. This could just be coincidence. If you know that you are good, then you should persevere and be as assertive as possible without being rude. Don't hesitate to call the agents at regular intervals as long as you are confident and courteous. The next job might be just around the corner. On the other hand, you should also be realistic. If you have been auditioning for two years unsuccessfully and have been heard by most of the agents, it might mean that you need to rethink your situation. You might need a few more years of study or you might simply not be good enough.

## Behaving on stage

The rules of conduct onstage (as well as theatre superstitions) that are to be found in practically every opera house in the world also exist in Germany; not only during performances, but at all times. The three most important rules are:
* Do not whistle on stage or in the wings. This superstition is so strong in Germany that you will be criticised for whistling in your dressing room or even in the corridor.
* Do not eat or drink on stage or in the wings.
* Do not wear coats, hats or any other outdoor clothing on stage or in the wings (unless, of course, it is for the role).
Most professionals in the theatre business take these rules very seriously. You might find them silly or unnecessary but if you do not learn to respect them, you do not belong on the professional stage.

Do not ask the advice of any amateur not actively working in the business! There are unfortunately a very large number of "camp followers" in this profession. They are often failed singers who have not made it themselves but always know best. They are over-critical of their working "colleagues" and they are very free with advice. Their advice is usually neither professional nor productive. The failed singers will often make other people (agents, conductors, stage directors) responsible for their own lack of success. Learn very soon in your career to discern between well-meant, objective and professional advice and the subjective half-baked opinions of the non-professional.

**4**

# The First Engagement

At last all your hard work has been rewarded and you're singing professionally in Germany. This could be as
* a member of a "studio"
* a soloist singing smaller parts in a big house
* a soloist singing anything from smaller to big roles in a small or middle-sized house
* a freelance singer
* a member of the opera chorus (see chapter 5)

## The Studio

The *studio* (or *das Junge Ensemble* as it is sometimes called) is a training program attached to some of the bigger opera houses in Germany. If you have just left opera school and feel that you still lack confidence or experience to sing medium-sized or major roles, then this is an interesting and productive possibility. Here you will be given the chance to get to know the workings of a fully professional opera house in a protected environment. You will work with the coaches, sing small roles and receive a salary. It is a great opportunity to observe the professionals at work and to see how an opera production comes into being. Unfortunately, there are not many such studios in Germany. They are not always mentioned in the *Bühnenjahrbuch*, and the number of available studios fluctuates from year to year. Sometimes new ones open up and sometimes established ones may close. The best is to ask your agent about them or contact the larger opera houses like Hamburg, Berlin, Düsseldorf, Cologne, Dresden and Munich.

Advantages

## 4 ◆ The First Engagement

### Big or small roles?

Whether you sing big or small roles does not always depend on you. Usually one has to take what is offered. If however you do have the choice between singing the second *Fach* in an A or B house or the big *Fach* in a C or D house (see chapter 6 for the classification of opera houses), then you should consider certain factors.

**Advantages**

Advantages of starting with small roles in a big house:
* You will get to sing with renowned singers and can learn from them
* You can try out your vocal and acting abilities in roles that are not quite as exposed as the leading roles
* You get to know influential people and can make important contacts
* You can learn from working with excellent coaches, stage directors and conductors

**Disadvantages**

Disadvantages of singing small roles in a big house:
* You don't get to sing the roles of your *Fach*
* You can get stuck there longer than is good for you because the salary is relatively good

### Working as a freelance singer

This means that you are on your own. You will have to:
* Contact agents and opera houses personally on a regular basis
* Have a big repertoire of usable roles
* Be responsible for learning your roles and must arrive completely prepared
* Know the roles so well (musically and interpretatively) that you can take over a new production within short notice
* Know your roles in the original languages as well as in a German translation

- Own scores of all your roles
- Be well informed about the various traditional versions and cuts
- Be very flexible and be prepared to travel at a moment's notice
- Have strong nerves and manage stress well
- Learn the entire role without cuts. You might have some nasty surprises otherwise
- Know all the dialogues, no matter how old-fashioned they may seem to you

**Tip**

You might have to return to your home country (especially if you are not a resident of a European country) in between engagements to apply for a new visa and work permit.

**Guest appearance or guesting**

A contract for one specific production on a freelance basis is called *das Gastspiel*.

There are two kinds of *Gastspiele*.

- You can be given a contract for a new production. This means you will live in that particular city for a period of 4 to 8 weeks, depending on the rehearsal period and the number of performances.
- You may have to take over from a singer who has cancelled a performance. This is called *einspringen* (verb) – literally to "jump in". To do this you have to be so sure of the role that you can sing it in your sleep and fit into an unfamiliar production at a few hours' notice.

A singer who has decided to work on a freelance basis must be capable of doing both kinds of *Gastspiele*. The first is much easier and less stressful. For the second, you have to have a certain amount of stage experience and nerves of steel.

Jumping in!

# 4 ◆ The First Engagement

**Long guesting**

Rules for "guesting" in a new production:

- You will be expected to pay your own apartment, so consider this when negotiating your fee. Very often, the theatre will help you find a place to live.
- Take some black-and-white glossy photos and your résumé (in a language that will be understood) for the program and the press.
- Travel light. Don't pack all your elegant clothes and jewellery. You will need one elegant outfit for press conferences and the opening night and the rest of the time you will need comfortable rehearsal clothes.
- Pack your comfortable stage shoes and a set of good underwear (in case of see-through costumes!).
- If you guest in Italy, France or Spain you should at least have a working knowledge of the language.

**Tip**

Rehearsals for a new production can last anywhere from 4 to 6 weeks, depending on the demands of the stage director.

**Short guesting**

Rules for taking over at a short notice (*das Einspringen*):

- Usually it will be someone from the KBB (*das Künstlerische Betriebsbüro*) of an opera house who calls you because one of their singers has cancelled. This is sometimes at a very short notice. Ask them exactly which role it is. It has been known to happen that they confuse the "first lady" with the "second lady"!
- Ask them which version they are doing. For instance, they could be doing the "Fontainebleau" scene in *Don Carlos*, which is very often left out. Or, if you only know the Dresden version of *Tannhäuser* and the theatre performs the Paris version, you should know this beforehand. Some theatres like to present the complete versions of Mozart and Rossini operas. It can happen that you have to "jump in" for a Marcellina or a Basilio in *Le nozze di Figaro* and discover that you have to sing the aria, which is normally left out. Or, you could be asked to sing the Kostelnicka in *Jenůfa* and discover that you have to sing the Prague version with the aria in the first act.

- Make sure you know in which language the opera is sung. Some smaller houses still perform Italian and French operas in German. Make certain that you know the translation they are using, as there are very often two or three different German versions. Sometimes a theatre will write its own translation.
- Ask the *KBB* to book your hotel room, as in most cases the theatres get a discount. Sometimes the theatre will pay for the hotel, but mostly you are responsible for your own hotel expenses.
- Ask about the travel arrangements. Sometimes the theatre will book your flight, and sometimes you will have to do this yourself. In both cases, the theatre will pay your travelling expenses (unfortunately, this will also be taxed). You might have to pay in advance. Make copies of your train or air ticket to give to them for the reimbursement.
- Ask what the costume looks like in case your own "very comfortable" stage shoes fit in with the style.
- Have your measurements ready.
- When negotiating a fee, always let them make an offer first and then go up one notch. If this does not work, it means that the theatre really cannot pay more.

Make a list of things you will need to take on an unexpected *Gastspiel* and always have it ready in your desk drawer. Then you can be sure that you will not forget something important when you have to leave at a moments' notice.

Tip

Here is an example of what such a list could look like:
- Vocal score
- Portable keyboard
- Portable music player plus a recording of the role
- Stage shoes or special underclothes
- Your measurements
- Contact lenses (also a substitute pair)
- Mobile phone, plus charger
- Credit cards
- Passport

♦ Essential medication
♦ Special sleeping pillow
♦ Lucky charm or talisman
♦ Etc. etc. etc.

Tip
You will not have to bring your own make-up (*die Schminke*), as every German opera house has its own make-up artists (*der Maskenbildner/die Maskenbildnerin*) and they will not allow you to do your own make-up.

When you arrive at the theatre, the stage director's assistant (*der Regieassistent/die Regieassistentin*) will be waiting for you. You will then go for a costume fitting before rehearsing the part with the assistant and a pianist. You can consider yourself lucky if one of your stage colleagues turns up for this rehearsal.

It is better to "walk through" the staging on a rehearsal stage than to look at a video if you do not have time to do both. Your body will remember the moves more easily than when you have just looked at a video passively.

## Working as a soloist in an opera house

Thomas Hampson once said: "Nobody cares about your career more than you do."

This is an essential principle for a professional singer. Once you are a member of an opera house, you will be expected to take responsibility for your voice and performance level. This means working

The bass, Kurt Moll working with the conductor, Ivor Bolton

on your voice every day and never leaving out your vocal exercises before a rehearsal or performance. You will be expected to sing rehearsals and performances almost daily and building up your stamina is a foremost priority. You will be responsible for looking after your own mental and physical health and seeing that your immune system is in full working order. You will be expected to be reliable and punctual. You should be aware of your "place" in the scheme of things.

We know of a young baritone who had been given the chance of singing a small role in a production in a very important house. His colleagues were world-class. He turned up at the first ensemble rehearsal with the famous conductor and immediately announced that he had a cold and would not sing at all! The assistant conductor had to sing his part, which made it very difficult for the conductor as well as for the colleagues with the big roles who were all singing full voice. He might have felt a bit nervous at the thought of a first rehearsal under such daunting circumstances, but he should have pulled himself together, warmed up his voice carefully and at least have tried to sing as much as possible, instead of playing the divo. We hope that he at least used the rehearsal time to observe and learn from the great colleague who was singing the title role, as this was a *Fach* role that he would be singing one day.
On page 68 there is an example of the rehearsal schedule of a baritone in an average-sized German opera house.

**A case in point**

A singer in a *fest* (permanent) position might sing between 50 and 80 performances per season. In the average German house, you will find that you are only a little cog in a big wheel, where the make-up artist or technical assistant is just as important as the singer. You will learn how important it is to get on with the props master or your wigmaker. The stage door security man and your dresser are all professionals in their own right and are essential parts of a well-running machine. Playing the diva or divo will not get you very far, and

**Diva or Divo**

# 4 • The First Engagement

**Monday**
18.00–22.00 Stage rehearsal for the new production of
*Der Zigeunerbaron* (Homonay)

**Tuesday**
10.00–13.00 Stage rehearsal for *Der Zigeunerbaron*
19.00–23.00 Performance of *Carmen* (Dancairo)

**Wednesday**
10.00–13.00 Orchestra rehearsal (*die Sitzprobe*) for *Der
Zigeunerbaron*
19.00–22.00 Performance of *Don Pasquale* (Malatesta)

**Thursday**
10.00–16.00 Piano dress rehearsal for *Der Zigeunerbaron*
Evening free

**Friday**
11.00–13.00 Ensemble rehearsal with the conductor for
*La Traviata* (Baron Duphol)
17.00–18.00 Musical and stage corrections for *Der Zigeunerbaron*

**Saturday**
10.00–14.00 Orchestra dress rehearsal for *Zigeunerbaron*
17.00–18.00 Rehearsal with a new Violetta (due to cancella-
tion)
19.00–23.00 Performance of *La Traviata*

**Sunday**
Morning free
19.00–22.00 Performance of *Don Pasquale*

**Monday**
11.00–15.00 Final dress rehearsal for *Der Zigeunerbaron*
Evening free

**Tuesday**
Free

**Wednesday**
12.00–13.00 Musical coaching for the next role *La Bohème*
(Marcello)
19.00–23.00 Opening night of *Der Zigeunerbaron*

in fact will make you very unpopular! Singers have been known to lose their jobs because of "an attitude problem".

**Rivalry among colleagues**

As a permanent member of the company, you will probably have to sing parts that you are not happy with, or you might find that your colleague, singing the same *Fach* as you, has been cast in a role that you feel you should be doing. This is all part of the game, and the sooner you learn to make the best of the situation the quicker you will get on with your career. You will feel as if you are on a tightrope. On the one hand, you will be expected to show verve, individualistic talent and temperament on stage, but on the other hand you have to become part of the team in the everyday life of the theatre. You must do this on your own because the artistic management will not hold your hand. They will expect you to function as a reliable member of the company and do as you are told. Do not expect fairness. The opera company is not run according to individual needs and wishes and you will have to fit into the general organization.

**Feedback**

You will discover very soon that the only feedback you get might be criticism and that you will seldom receive praise. It is up to you to use every constructive criticism or feedback to improve your performance.

You will also find that a stage director will not have time to mollycoddle you during a production. He will give you an instruction and expect you to do it. If you feel that your acting skills are not up to it, it will be your responsibility to find an acting teacher able to tell you how to produce what is expected of you on stage. At the beginning of your career you will not have much opportunity for long debates with the director to tell him how you would like to play the part. The system does not allow time for this. You will be expected to do what the director wants, go home after every rehearsal, write down everything discussed during the day, practice the moves and then do them correctly the next day.

# 4 ◆ The First Engagement

As a soloist in an average German house, you must be available every day (seven days a week). The rehearsal plan (*der Probenplan*) for tomorrow is usually only posted the afternoon before. This means that you will not be able to plan your private life ahead of time. You will only find out at midday what you are rehearsing the next day. It could be a solo musical call, or it could be a staging or ensemble rehearsal for the opera being prepared at the moment. If you are not in the current production, you might have slightly more free time but you will still be working on your repertoire for later in the season. Apart from that, you might be covering (understudying) a part and have to be available in case your colleague cancels. This can happen as late as midday on the day of a performance. It is your duty to see that you can be reached every day.

Singers have been fired because of not having their mobile phones on when out shopping or visiting friends and not being able to get back in time to save a performance.

**Leave**

According to your contract, you are allowed a certain amount of leave during a season if you receive an offer to sing elsewhere. In this case, you must apply for leave (*der Urlaub*) officially, and it is always possible that it may not be granted if you are needed in your own house. The theatre is under no obligation to give you leave. This can be very frustrating for a young ambitious singer. It may happen that you are singing the second priest in *Die Zauberflöte*, and you get an offer to sing Papageno in another house. You will not be allowed to accept the offer because you are getting paid to sing whatever you are given in your own house. The best way to manage these frustrations is to tell yourself that you are learning many other things in your first job and that you have to get through these "learning years" with grace. If you are good enough, the bigger roles will not run away. They will come your way later. Don't be impatient.

**Tip**

Try to find a friend you can trust in the theatre who will give you objective and professional advice when you have a problem. This could be an experienced singing colleague, a stage director's assistant or a coach.

You need three basic requirements to survive in the German theatre system:  **Hard skills**
* A high level of singing and musical skills
* Finely honed acting skills
* Management skills for the profession

The first two you learn at opera school. The rules of the profession you have to learn yourself. Playing the professional game and knowing how to behave can be compared to general corporate rules. Learn how to run your career like a business.

The same rules that apply in other professions must also be applied in the theatre:  **Soft skills**
* Efficiency
* Discipline
* Punctuality
* Reliability
* Availability
* Professionalism

Learn the rules of professional behaviour quickly. If you are late for rehearsals, do not know your work, cancel too often, argue too often with conductors or stage directors, gossip in the cafeteria and are generally disorganized and unreliable, you will very soon get a bad reputation in the business.

> Be realistic about your capabilities, but also know your limits. For instance, don't accept too many concerts or roles and then find out too late that you can't manage all of them. Don't sing roles that are too difficult or too big for you.

The conductor Fabio Luisi (Metropolitan Opera New York, Vienna State Opera and Salzburg Festival), said in an interview: "The problem is that every one is in such a hurry nowadays. In the past, everyone started in small regional houses and let their careers develop gradually by not singing the major roles right away and by having a sort of 'humility' about the roles they learned and sang. They spent their whole lives working on their technique, style, and realization of a role. Today people come out of nowhere and sing the major roles at major houses without really understanding the roles or being able to sing them. After a few years, they just disappear from the operatic stage. I think this practice is immoral towards the art, the singers and the audience. The responsibility lies with the general managers, agents, record companies, and often with the conductors because they no longer take the time anymore to allow a singer to develop. Instead they are always on the lookout for young and interesting 'new blood'." (Opernwelt, 2001, 7)

## The organization of an average German opera house

**Hierarchical structure**

An opera house is a hierarchical structure. Every person has his or her place and function in it, and the system is fundamentally autocratic. The *Intendant* may hire and fire whenever and whomever he wants to. The assertion that an artist "is not artistically compatible with the concept of the house" is generally considered a valid and legal ground for getting rid of a singer. In the German opera world, one does not talk about "firing" a singer, because the contracts are only valid for a restricted period of time (usually one or two seasons). You will simply be told that your contract has not been renewed. There is not very much you can do about this (see chapter 6).

A young singer must learn how the hierarchy works and how he or she should behave within this structure.

**The management**

Every opera house is run by:
* an artistic director (*der Intendant/die Intendantin*)
* a musical director (*der Generalmusikdirektor/die Generalmusikdirektorin, GMD*)
* an administrative director (*der Verwaltungsdirektor/die Verwaltungsdirektorin*)

In rare cases, the *Generalmusikdirektor* (*GMD*) can also be the *Intendant*.

The *Intendant* and *GMD* are artistically responsible for planning the repertoire (*der Spielplan*). They will then hire a director, a set and costume designer and (in the larger houses) a conductor for each opera. Productions in smaller houses will be conducted by the staff conductors (*der Kapellmeister/die Kapellmeisterin*) of which there are usually at least two. Very often, the *Intendant* will direct one or two operas himself and the *GMD* always chooses his own conducting repertoire, as well as allocating the remaining conducting assignments. The casting is done by the artistic heads. This is again the *Intendant*, and *GMD*, and in some cases, the director and the conductor of the specific piece.

Before the stage rehearsals begin, the singers learn their roles individually with a coach and finally the head of music will call ensemble rehearsals. This is particularly important in Mozart and Rossini operas where the recitatives and ensembles need to be rehearsed like clockwork. In the meantime, the stage director will have delivered his concept to the workshops. They will start building the sets and making the costumes, wigs, furniture and props. The lighting department starts designing the lighting and the production team starts making the rehearsal schedules for the stage rehearsals.

## The music coach

**Important artistic partner**

The coach is responsible for style, musicality, interpretation, phrasing and diction. He is not there to teach you the notes. This you have to do by yourself. A good coach is a specialist who can play the piano score so well that the singer can hear what the orchestra will be doing. He knows which instruments are important and what you should listen for. He can also help you to develop the right vocal sound for the specific role. Not only can a good coach help you with the correct pronunciation but he also knows the dramatic demands of each role and can help you find the right emotion and colour. He will later play for the staging rehearsals and is one of the most important artistic partners in preparing your role.

**Tip**

If you have the feeling that the coach with whom you are preparing your role is not up to the standard you can expect, we suggest that you invest the time and money to study your role with an expert, even if he is in another city. Once you have learnt a role properly, it will last you for your whole professional life.

## The head of the music staff

Once the ensemble rehearsals start, they will be led by the head of the music staff (*der Studienleiter/die Studienleiterin*) or the conductor. The *Studienleiter* is the direct link between the conductor and the coaches and singers. He organizes the musical rehearsal schedules. In some houses he is also responsible for compiling the daily rehearsal plans which include staging calls. In the bigger houses there is a special office called *die Regiekanzlei* where the rehearsal schedules are coordinated.

The *Studienleiter* has to see to it that the quality of the musical preparation is always as high as possible. He and the other coaches are also responsible for conducting the staging rehearsals when the conductor is not available. The *Studienleiter* knows every singer in the house and is often asked to give casting advice.

> The *Studienleiter* is not only a coach and a good organizer, but is also generally known as the musical conscience of the house.

**Staging rehearsal**

The next step in the rehearsal sequence will be the staging rehearsals (*die szenische Probe*) on a rehearsal stage. You will not have the set or costumes, and will be given rehearsal costumes and makeshift props. This is a good opportunity to use your imagination in creating the inner feeling for a role. Look at the costume and set designs well ahead of time because this will help you to get into the role.

The first rehearsal is normally preceded by a discussion (*das Konzeptionsgespräch*) where the production team will explain their concept of the piece. Here the stage director, set and costume designers have the opportunity to explain how they work and what their main creative impetus is.

The director usually has one or two assistants (*der Regieassistent/die Regieassistentin*) depending on the size of the house. Also in attendance will be a pianist, a rehearsal conductor, the prompter, the stage manager and various members of the technical staff responsible for props, costumes, etc. In Germany, most rehearsals start at 10.00 and will last until 13.00 or 14.00. There is usually an afternoon break (union rules). The evening rehearsals are normally from 17.00 till 22.00.

## The stage director

Stage directors (*der Regisseur/die Regisseurin*) are individualists and can be as different from one another as singers are different from one another. You will find the autocratic type who has every single move written down before the rehearsals start, and expects the singers to do exactly as they are told without any discussion. Then you may find the so-called spontaneous type, who comes with a flexible concept and will expect the singers to contribute to the creative process. Some singers prefer to be told what to do whilst others find it very exciting to participate in creating a role. Both methods can be valid and successful, but you will have to be flexible and be able to work in both types of environments, as long as your vocal production is not hampered. You might find that your own artistic horizon will be widened by a new approach that you have never thought of before. However, if you find that you are having problems accepting the working method or creative concept of a particular stage director, do not criticize or complain during a rehearsal or in front of the colleagues. It is always a better idea to find a quiet moment in which to speak to the stage director privately, voicing your difficulties in a calm and rational way. If this does not work, you will have to decide what is best for your career. As a member of a company, it might not be a good idea to refuse to do the part. You might just have to grin and bear it unless you feel that your voice is going to be harmed by what you have to do.

### The stage director's assistant

The stage director's assistants (*der Regieassistent/die Regieassistentin*) have to assist the stage director in every way by organizing the rehearsals and co-ordinating the contact between the director and the technical staff. They are also responsible for making detailed notes in the production book recording every move and technical directive on stage.

The assistant has to see to it that the new singers are "placed" into an existing production within a few days without losing the spirit or basic concept of the original production. This is difficult and responsible work.

The assistant is responsible for looking after the production once the director has left. He has to revive it in subsequent seasons exactly the way the director wanted it. In bigger houses, the productions are recreated three or four times per season over a long period of time.

## The stage manager

Another indispensable member of the team is the stage manager (*der Inspizient/die Inspizientin*). He has to see to it that everything runs smoothly and efficiently on stage and he should be the calmest person on the team. He will attend the rehearsals in order to note down exactly what should be happening on stage at every given moment. He reads music perfectly and cues the singers' entrances and also gives lighting and other technical cues. On the night of a performance, he is the boss. When he starts giving the calls ("thirty minutes, please!") things are getting serious and nerves start fluttering. The stage manager has to make sure that the singers are waiting in the wings before their entrances and has to be fully aware of everything happening on stage. He is responsible for law and order and even has the power to throw the stage director out if he starts disturbing the peace! The stage director gives the production into the hands of the stage manager on the opening night. Some directors have great difficulty letting go of their "creation" and might start telling singers and technicians to make changes five minutes before the curtain goes up. This will not be allowed by the "boss".

Even though the stage manager has to call you in time for your entrance, you must not rely on this and always have to see to it that you know when to go on stage. A professional singer will always report to the stage manager as soon as he is on the stage. It is also a very good idea to tell your dresser if you are going to use the elevator or go to the toilet. Stuck elevators or toilet doors have been known to happen!

Tip

**77**

# 4 • The First Engagement

## The prompter

A profession with
tradition

Another essential member of the stage team is the opera prompter (*der Souffleur/die Souffleuse*). This is a very specific profession usually found only in German-speaking (including Austria and Switzerland) and Italian opera houses. The prompter sits in the prompt box, which is usually a low box in front of the stage. This tradition comes from straight theatre and you have all seen it in the movies. The opera prompter is usually a musician who can read the piano score perfectly, can speak all the sung languages and is proficient in giving the cues before every line. The prompter does not have to sing, but speaks the first few words of every spoken or sung line exactly one beat before you have to sing or speak it. This has to be articulated loudly and clearly enough for the singers to hear but not so loud as to be heard in the auditorium! Some prompters also conduct and can give you musical cues if necessary. The prompter is particularly valuable during rehearsals because he or she can help you memorize the text.

The prompter's desk

## The props master or mistress

Another important artistic partner is the props master or props mistress (*der Requisiteur/die Requisiteurin*). He or she makes or provides the objects that you will be handling on stage such as flowers, baskets, glasses, plates, letters, bottles, candlesticks, whips, swords, guns, etc.

The props master has to attend all rehearsals and is then responsible for providing the necessary props (properties). During the rehearsals, he will see to it that you have rehearsal props and will provide the original props at the first dress rehearsal. The props department is not responsible for costume props such as handbags, fans, parasols, shawls or capes – these are provided by the costume department. During a performance, your dresser (*der Garderobier/die Garderobiere*) is responsible for giving you your costume props or seeing to it that they are set on stage, if you need them there.

A singer should appreciate the work of the props department. The way the props are made can very much influence your performance. Ask them to give you rehearsal props that have the same weight and size as the originals to avoid possible unpleasant surprises at the first dress rehearsal. Wine or beer bottles are filled with a substitute liquid, mostly raspberry or apple juice. If you happen to be allergic to anything, please inform them in good time.

Although the props department will lay everything onto the props table in the wings before the performance, the singer-performer is always responsible for checking the props. You cannot make the props department responsible if an important piece is not ready for you when you go on stage. Don't forget to put your props back before you leave the stage! The same applies for the costume props, which should be returned to your dresser after use.

Tip

For the next rehearsal phase, the production moves to the main stage. This is exciting, because you start getting a feel-

**Rehearsals on the main stage**

**79**

ing for the dimensions of the stage and auditorium – even if the original set is not yet ready.

**Costume fitting**

At this point you will be called to the costume department (*die Kostümabteilung* or *die Schneiderei*) for a costume fitting. The designer as well as the seamstress (*die Schneiderin*) or the tailor (*der Schneider*) will attend, and this is the time to find out whether you feel comfortable in the costume. You

Siegfried Jerusalem at
a costume fitting

should try out all the physical moves that are expected of you in your role (i. e. sitting down, dancing, climbing ladders, or lifting your arms), so that they can suggest changes, if necessary. If you need a pocket for an important prop or the neckline is so high that your larynx feels restricted, this is the time to tell them. Are the shoes comfortable? Do you have a long train that is impossible to work with? You may possibly not feel very happy with the design, because it does not flatter you. This you will not be able to change, because the concept is already decided upon. You should remember that you are not a private person on stage. You are playing a role that is possibly completely different from your private self. This is what professionalism is all about – being the person on stage! The only exception to this is if the designer or director expects you to be naked on stage, and in this case it is acceptable to refuse. The problem might be solved by wearing a flesh-coloured leotard (body stocking).

Performing naked has been known to happen on German opera stages. In June 2004, the Catalan director, Calixto Bieito, directed a production of *Die Entführung aus dem Serail* in the *Komische Oper Berlin*, where the entire cast (men and women) were stark naked! They also had to perform rape scenes and orgies. There were obviously enough singers who were prepared to do this. It is a matter of taste whether such a production is valid or aesthetic.

After your costume fitting you should ask the designer to allow you to use parts of the original costume at the rehearsals. This is especially important with cloaks, trains and shoes. Usually, the costume department wants to protect the costumes and prefers not to make them available before the first dress rehearsal. If that is the case, then you should ask them to make you a similar cloak or train for the rehearsals. We suggest however that you insist on using the original shoes for every rehearsal, as this is very important for your posture, walk and interpretation.

**Tips**

• In the English theatre one speaks of prompt side – the left side of the stage seen from the performer's point of view, and OP (opposite prompt) side – the right side of the stage seen from the performer's point of view. When the director in Germany asks you to go to the right side of the stage (*Bühne*

# 4 ◆ The First Engagement

The metamorphosis of an opera singer

*rechts*), he means right as seen from 'his' point of view. So left stage (*Bühne links*) will be the left side of the stage as seen from the auditorium.

◆ There is no expression for upstage and downstage in German. The director will say "*gehen Sie nach hinten*" (go back or upstage) or "*kommen Sie nach vorne*" (come forward or downstage). The wonderful expression "upstaging" someone has no equivalent in German, although it is done just as often as anywhere else!

## Die Sitzprobe

After a few rehearsals on stage, you will be called to an orchestra rehearsal without staging (*die Sitzprobe*, also called *italiana* or *generale* in other European countries). This is the first rehearsal with the orchestra and takes place either on-stage or in the orchestra rehearsal room. The singers sit behind the orchestra and should have their scores with them. Even if you have memorized every note, you will still want to take notes. Also, the conductor will be jumping back and forth and will give you the bar numbers when he repeats a section. You will be expected to sing out at the *Sitzprobe*. As it is usually at 10.00 in the morning, you might want to go to bed early the night before! The *Sitzprobe* is a good opportunity to dress well – it will make you feel good after all those rehearsals on dusty stages.

**82**

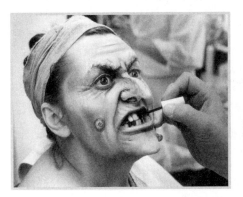

The next step is usually the piano dress rehearsal (*die Kla-vierhauptprobe* or *die Schlussprobe*). This rehearsal belongs to the director, and as there is no orchestra in the pit (just a piano), he will use the opportunity to solve any technical problems regarding costume, props, set changes, lighting, etc. The singers are well advised to save their voices because it is a long rehearsal and the emphasis will be on technical stage details and not the music. There will be much repetition. The singers use this rehearsal to get used to their costumes. The dressers (*die Garderobieren*, pl) have to practice quick costume changes and the make-up department (*die Maske*) has to find out how long it takes to make up the singers.

**The piano dress rehearsal**

Before the final technical rehearsal, the singers should arrive at least one and a half hours before curtain-up because of possible hitches with costumes and make-up.

Then the stage rehearsals with orchestra (*die Bühnenorchesterprobe*, abbr. *BO*) start. A *BO* will never last more than three hours because of orchestra union rules unless an exception has been agreed upon. The conductor is in charge and the singers must sing out. They will again wear rehearsal clothes and will probably concentrate more on their singing than on acting details. The stage director may not interfere and is usually very frustrated because he sees his production falling to pieces! But then come the dress rehearsals with orchestra and everything falls into place again.

**The stage rehearsal with orchestra**

## The conductor

In this section, we will again use the "he" form (see Foreword) when talking about the conductor (*der Dirigent/die Dirigentin*), although we are well aware of the fact that there are many competent female opera conductors in Germany.

**The ideal opera conductor**

The ideal opera conductor knows the opera so well that he can concentrate on just making music. He knows how the singing voice functions, listens to the singers and is involved in the drama that is happening on stage. He prepares the singers in ensemble rehearsals and conducts the staging rehearsals so that he learns what the singers need and they learn what he wants. He supports the singers by breathing with them and through accompanying them, enables them to be free. Unfortunately, some conductors are exactly the opposite. They are autocratic, don't listen to the singers, and sometimes arrive for rehearsals on the day of the first orchestral rehearsal, leaving the work of fusing the ensemble into a whole to the coaches. Nonetheless, an inexperienced singer must learn to listen to the conductor and accept his musical concept. It's a case of give and take – through teamwork one can achieve much more than through insisting on your own (not always correct) tempi or interpretation. The first thing a young singer has to learn is to look at the conductor at all times. Doing this without it being too noticeable is an art not easily come by. You will be so distracted by other things that you will have to force yourself at every rehearsal (and especially every performance) to look at the conductor. This can be either directly, out of the corner of your eye, or in the monitor (TV set in the wings). This is not easy when you are in the middle of a love scene! Experienced singers know how to look passionate while looking over their heads of their stage lovers at the monitor in the wings!

**The first dress rehearsal**

With the first dress rehearsal (*die Hauptprobe*), we get down to the nitty gritty. Now you have the set, costumes, lighting and orchestra. For the singers, this can be compared to a performance, and every technician, make-up artist, dresser and props person does his or her best to create that feeling of magic that one always feels when a performance is underway. The director and the conductor try not to interrupt a scene unless something goes very wrong. There will be photographers in the auditorium and sometimes even television teams. The conductor and stage director make notes with the help of their assistants and there will be a brainstorming (die Kritik) after the rehearsal for everybody for last-minute changes and instructions. Even if you only sang in the first scene, you have to stay on for the Kritik unless you have been told by the assistants that you will not be needed.

> Never leave the theatre without reporting to the stage manager and the musical assistants.

**The final dress rehearsal**

The final dress rehearsal (die Generalprobe) is to all intents and purposes the first performance and most singers start feeling stage fright at this point. There will be no interruptions and very often there will be a selected audience – mostly colleagues, friends, family members or music students.

> It is an old theatre tradition to believe that when things go wrong at the Generalprobe the opening night will be perfect!

**The opening night**

The opening night (die Premiere) is the culmination of a long and intensive preparation period. There is a feeling of magic in the air and everybody feels excited about presenting a new creation that has never been seen before. This experience can be terrifying but also highly stimulating. The singers are lifted into a new dimension of consciousness and the actual physical singing-process becomes unimportant as one "becomes" the character. All private thoughts recede into the background and the rehearsed moves become alive. You instinctively bond and communicate with the audience on a near-spiritual level.

During the intensive preparation for a role, most singers find it difficult to combine their private lives with the life of the character they are playing. You are absolutely absorbed in

**85**

the character and even at night your lines run through your head. The priorities lie with your work and you do not have so much time for your family. Your family has to understand this and support you. On the other hand, it is also important to stay based in your everyday reality.

Performing with real water (Sabine Hogrefe as Tatjana in *Evgeny Onegin*)

## Professional behaviour in everyday theatre life

* Don't say negative things about colleagues. If you feel that a colleague is not up to standard, then tell your partner or a trusted friend at home, but do not express your negative opinions in the theatre. Keep out of gossip and intrigues involving colleagues or you will soon find yourself with a bad reputation.
* Never talk about money! Don't tell people what you are earning. This is not considered good form.
* Don't discuss job offers before the contract has been signed. A contract that is still being negotiated is called *ein ungelegtes Ei* (an unlaid egg!)
* Don't make a nuisance of yourself by telling the *KBB* which roles you want to sing. If you think they do not appreciate you, ask the *Studienleiter* to work the role with you and then give you his objective advice. Then ask for an audition.
* Be punctual. Never arrive late for a rehearsal. This means that you have to arrive in time to warm up your voice and put on your rehearsal clothes. If

you are understudying a part and are expected to sit and watch, see that you are ready to "jump in". This also means that you have to warm up your voice.

* If you have a few minutes off during a rehearsal, show your interest by behaving quietly and paying attention. Don't sit and read, do crossword puzzles, eat or talk loudly because this will disturb the concentration of the stage director or singers on stage. Don't forget to turn off your cell phone!

* Show your interest by watching the scenes in which you are not participating. You might learn many things about your character.

> Even if the score belongs to you, we recommend that you make your notes with a soft pencil. You might be doing a new production in a few years' time and have to erase the old one.

* Always have your score with you and make notes of every new move. Practice the moves at home before the next rehearsal. Nothing is worse than a singer who makes the same mistakes repeatedly. In Germany, you will often be expected to repeat the opera a year later. There won't be many rehearsals and you will need your notes.

* When the stage director is showing you what he wants, do not stand behind him but move forward where you can see him clearly.

* Sometimes rehearsals can become boring because scenes are repeated often. You should still be involved and show your interest for the sake of the colleagues who might need to rehearse more often. You can always learn something, even if you just try out your body language or posture in different ways.

* Don't eat or whistle at a rehearsal. Singers are particularly superstitious about whistling. This is not even allowed in the dressing rooms or corridors.

* Don't clutter every chair with your coat or bags.

* Don't wear strong perfume. Strong scents make it hard for some singers to breathe.

* Dress appropriately. Wear rehearsal clothes that are suitable for the role, and under no circumstances should you

wear tons of jewellery. Wearing shorts or dressing provocatively is also not acceptable, unless it has something to do with the role.

## Professional behaviour at performances

**Arrive at the theatre on time**

It is important for you and your colleagues to arrive at the theatre on time. There is a rule that you have to be in your dressing-room at least half an hour before the performance, unless you are only in the second half of the opera after the intermission. Then you must be there half an hour before the intermission. If you are not on time, the dressers have to report it to the stage manager. We suggest that you come as early as possible, especially if there are many soloists who have to be made up. There might be a pile-up and this will only make you nervous. Some singers like to warm up their voices in the theatre and give themselves enough time to go through their role again. If you are not on time, you might find that all the music rooms are occupied.

**Being a good colleague**

Very often you will have to share a dressing room. This can be unpleasant for all parties concerned unless everybody behaves considerately. Do not use strong perfume, do not eat garlic before a performance and do not sing in the dressing-room! It is also considered bad form to receive friends and members of your family before or during a performance. They do not belong backstage. Even if you do have your own dressing room, it could be more distracting than you think to have to entertain people who are not directly involved in the production.

Use the time before your entrance to be still and concentrate totally on mobilizing your creative powers. While you are being made up, you should not chat or gossip with the make-up artist (*die Maskenbildnerin/der Maskenbildner*) but rather use the time to get into your character.

Remember to take off your personal jewellery and wrist-watch. Do this deliberately to help yourself move from the private person into the stage person.

If you have a quick costume change behind the scenes, keep calm and let the dressers do their work. The more hectic and excited you get, the longer it will take.

Test your voice and general condition early on the morning of a performance and let the theatre know promptly if you have to cancel. The latest you are allowed to cancel is noon on the day of the performance, but you usually know before-hand if you are incapable of singing and it would be more considerate to let the KBB know right away so that they can find a replacement more easily.

## The audience

The famous acting teacher Viola Spolin says: "The audience is the most revered member of the theatre. Without an audience there is no theatre. Every technique learned by the actor, every curtain, every flat on the stage, every careful analysis by the director, every coordinated scene, is for the enjoyment of the audience. They are our guests, our evalua-tors, and the last spoke in the wheel which can then begin to roll. They make the performance meaningful."
You would not be standing on stage if it were not for the many faithful opera lovers who regularly spend time and money to experience the great works in a live performance. Thank heavens there always seems to be a new generation of fans who fall in love with an art form that is considered by many people to be totally antiquated! Roaring applause or a stand-ing ovation is one of the most positive experiences that can happen to an opera singer. It inspires you and carries you forth on a wave of love and acceptance. The opposite is also possible. There are few singers who have not had the nasty

**89**

experience of being booed at some point in their career. This calls for professional behaviour. Do not show the audience that you are deeply hurt or feel insulted. Carry it off with grace even if you are seething inside. The thing to do afterwards is to think about the reason why it happened. It could be because you were not as good as you could have been and should reconsider the way you act and sing the role. But very often an audience is dissatisfied with the role conception or the production and you have to bear the brunt of their displeasure. Try not to let this experience upset you too much. Many good singers have been booed before you.

## At the stage door

After a performance, some opera lovers tend to gather at the stage door to meet their idols. In Germany they are not allowed to go into the dressing-rooms and therefore are prepared to wait outside for hours. Be friendly and give them some of your time. Often they will want your autograph (*das Autogramm*) in their program or a signed photo (*das Autogrammfoto*) and it is a good idea to have some ready. Most of them appreciate it immensely if you are prepared to take time for a chat. Don't forget that this is where your bread-and-butter comes from. It is important to remember not to talk negatively about colleagues and not to divulge inside information at the stage door. It is also not professional to discuss details of your private life.

At this point we should say a few words about the "opera fan". The word originates from "fanatic" and describes a certain portion of the audience who is particularly and intensively concerned with opera. On the one hand they can be very enthusiastic and it can be a pleasure to talk to them, and on the other hand they can very easily become so carried away that they cannot discriminate between appropriate and inappropriate behaviour. They become unrealistic about their place in the order of things and are inclined to overstep the mark.

These fans can even become dangerous and it is important that you treat them with respect but keep them at a distance; otherwise, they could invade your private life in an unpleasant and undesired way.

## Criticism

Apart from the audience, your performance will always be under scrutiny from the directors or your colleagues. They will also give their opinions – to your face or among themselves. Sometimes it will be positive and constructive criticism that should be taken seriously, and at other times, it will be vindictive and hurtful. Your best critic should always be yourself. Rely on your instincts to discriminate between helpful and destructive criticism.

**Constructive or destructive criticism?**

Then you also have to contend with criticism in the press. This can be devastating or ecstatic, depending on the critic of course. Before you take any press reviews seriously, it is important to know whether the writer is a professional who has thorough knowledge of the material. If what they write

Coping with criticism

is objective and seems to be well informed and discerning, you should give it some thought. Be open to ideas and try to analyze if there is something you might want to change in your performance. Other critics who write cynically or destructively are often failed artists themselves and should be ignored. It is considered bad form to write to the critic or the newspaper voicing your anger. It is far more professional to ignore it.

When you meet critics or members of the press personally (for interviews or at receptions), be very careful what you say. Be friendly, but discreet, and don't ever talk about conflicts between colleagues or insider knowledge that has not

Remember: a singer needs the press but can very quickly become its victim.

been made public yet. This is unprofessional and would be considered an act of disloyalty by your employer. Depending on how serious your indiscretion is, it could even jeopardize your job.

## Star quality

Sometimes a singer becomes a star overnight and is adored by the press and the public. Insiders often feel that this is

A radiant personality or charisma that reaches the hearts of the listeners is one of the most important attributes an artist could have.

unfair, as other singers who sing just as well (or even better), are not given such attention. What one forgets is that invisible and magic thing called "star quality" (*das gewisse Etwas*). This is difficult to define, because it is something that happens between the singer and the audience.

It operates on an invisible emotional level and is often more important than singing every note correctly or having a perfect vocal technique.

Sometimes an envious colleague will say, "she slept with the director" or "he just has a good public relations manager" but these things can only bring you part of the way – in the end you have to deliver the goods by enchanting your audiences.

# 5

# Singing in the Chorus

Every opera house in Germany has a professional chorus which is as important as the orchestra and is similar in its organization.

The decision to join an opera chorus must be made very consciously. Chorus singers are not failed soloists, and the quality of the applicants has reached a high standard, especially in the middle and the bigger houses. We do not recommend joining a chorus if you are still striving for a solo career. Going into a solo career after having sung in the chorus is very difficult and is usually doomed to failure.

Besides, it would be unfair towards your colleagues and the chorus master to leave a chorus after only a short while.

# 5 • Singing in the Chorus

The general rule is: A good chorus singer does not become a successful soloist – but a successful soloist can become a good chorus singer.

The chorus assistants invest a good deal of time in helping you build up the repertoire and putting you into existing complicated productions – a process which could take at least one season, depending on your experience.

## Requirements for singing in an opera chorus

* A stable singing technique
* Musicality
* Acting and dancing talent
* Discipline and stamina
* Fitness
* A pleasant appearance
* Good knowledge of German
* Basic knowledge of Italian and French
* Team spirit
* Being prepared to subordinate your voice to the specific sound of the chorus

**Solid vocal technique**

You should be able to sing in completely different styles within a few hours. You might start the morning with rehearsals for an operetta or a musical, and end the day with Mozart, Wagner or Verdi on stage. Your vocal technique must therefore be solid and flexible and your working-discipline of a high standard to cope with all these demands.

**Acting skills**

Although acting talent is not the topmost priority for a chorus job, you will need at least a few basic acting skills. No one can "hide" behind a colleague on stage, irrespective of the house size. You will always be seen by the audience.

Dancing also belongs to the basic acting skills and you will have to be able to dance a Viennese waltz, a minuet or a polka, not to mention the choreography suited for operetta or musicals. Look at the repertoire in German opera houses – you will find many operettas, musicals and operas with dance scenes!

Chorus work demands stamina, discipline and self-manage-ment. It will be up to you to maintain your voice. Do your exercises and work with your singing teacher regularly; above all, always warm up before a rehearsal or performance. You won't get any feedback from outside, and you can't always hear yourself while singing in a group.

**Stamina, discipline and self-management**

* Singers who have studied choral singing
* Singers who have studied to be soloists
* Singers who already have a position in an opera house as soloists

**Who is eligible for an opera chorus?**

Few singers know if they will want to become a member of an opera chorus at the start of their career. If you are not sure about a solo or chorus career choice don't tie yourself down too early. Those, however, who want to specialize right from the start will be able to study choral singing as a subject at certain universities in Germany. You will find the information on the Internet.

Becoming lazy is one of the greatest dangers in a chorus. Be aware of it and work against it right from the start. Give any undisciplined and sloppy colleagues a wide berth!

* You like chorus work
* You want financial and social security
* You find it a better way to combine job and family
* You suffer from stage fright as a soloist
* You learn that your voice is not adequate for a solo career, or is not strong enough to be heard over an orchestra
* You might not have the personality necessary for solo singing

**Good reasons for joining an opera chorus**

# 5 ◆ Singing in the Chorus

## Applying for a position

You should send your application directly to the opera house. Write to the chorus office (*das Chorbüro*). Chorus jobs are also advertised in the journals *Bühnengenossenschaft* and *Oper und Tanz* or on the websites of the opera houses. The only agency in Germany for finding chorus jobs is the state agency *ZBF* (*Zentrale Bühnen-, Fernseh- und Filmvermittlung*) in Cologne. The application for a chorus job is similar to that of a solo position.

**Tips**

◆ When you apply you should give a sound reason why you want to join a chorus.

Bad reasons would be "I am still not good enough for a solo position" or "I auditioned for solo jobs but couldn't get one". If you want to say that your voice is not strong enough for a solo job turn it into a positive statement, i.e. "I think my voice is especially qualified for chorus work".

◆ Chorus masters, especially those in bigger houses, like to employ experienced singers who have come out of smaller chorus or solo positions. Nowadays the standard is very high and your voice must be in an absolutely perfect condition with a well-functioning and flexible vocal technique!

◆ Many chorus masters hold informative auditions (*das Vorsingen zur Information*). The only persons involved are you and the chorus master, who will be able to inform you about your chances and whether your standard is good enough for a chorus work.

The voice types in a chorus differ from those of the soloists:

| First Soprano | *Sopran I* |
|---|---|
| Second Soprano | *Sopran II* |
| First Alto | *Alt I* |
| Second Alto | *Alt II* |
| First Tenor | *Tenor I* |
| Second Tenor | *Tenor II* |
| First Bass | *Bass I* |
| Second Bass | *Bass II* |

There is no mezzo-soprano or baritone in a chorus. A high mezzo would be put into *Sopran II*, a normal mezzo in *Alt I*, a high baritone into *Tenor II*, and a normal baritone into *Bass I*.

### Your application should contain the following documents
◆ A letter of application
◆ Your repertoire list (solo and chorus parts)

* A photo
* Your résumé (CV). You should mention all professional experience, such as any solo or chorus work on stage or in a concert choir of professional standard

## Age limit

The age limit differs slightly from house to house, depending on current supply and demand, as well as the practical experience of the individual applicant.

The following limits are generally valid:

| | |
|---|---|
| *Sopran I* and *II* | up to 32 |
| *Bass I, Alt I* | up to 34 |
| *Alt II* | up to 38 |
| *Bass II* | up to 40 |
| *Tenor I* and *II* | up to 40 |

## Auditioning

You will need at least five opera arias which suit your voice type. One must be in German. You can include an aria from an oratorio. Do not include *Lieder.* If the opera house also performs operettas and musicals you can add one or two appropriate arias or songs. Some chorus masters will want to hear a piece from the chorus repertoire.

**What to prepare**

Be prepared to do a musicianship and sight-reading test. At some houses they have compulsory arias (*das Pflichtstück*) for certain voice types. A typical example for a second alto position would be Magdalena's "O holde Jugendtage" from Wilhelm Kienzl's now-forgotten opera *Der Evangelimann*.

If you receive an invitation to audition for a chorus you should ask what will be expected of you. This can differ from chorus to chorus.

A chorus audition will take place in the presence of the chorus master and the chosen representatives of the chorus (*der Chorvorstand*).

# 5 ◆ Singing in the Chorus

## What else to do

◆ While studying you should join the extra or ad hoc chorus (*der Extrachor*) of the nearest opera house. It'll be a useful experience and you can make yourself known as a good and reliable chorus singer. It is easier for a member of an ad hoc chorus to find a permanent position later.

◆ As a beginner, you should start in a smaller house to let your voice develop and build up a repertoire.

◆ At the *Staatstheater Stuttgart* you could join the training program for young professional chorus singers (*das Chor-eleven-Programm*). For further information, look at www.staatstheater.stuttgart.de.

The *Semper Oper Dresden* also offers a training program called "*Das Opernchorstudio*". Look under www.semperoper.de.

◆ The *Festival d'Aix-en-Provence* invites the *Europa-Chor-akademie* for the chorus work in their opera productions. The stage training you will receive there can be very valuable for your future in a chorus. Look at www.festival-aix.com/academie/ or www.europachorakademie.de.

◆ The *Schleswig-Holstein Musikfestival* organizes the *Chor-akademie* which takes place every summer. This is an advanced vocational training for young singers. They primarily sing concert repertoire, but it is definitely also a good training for opera singers. Look at www.shmf.de.

◆ In a chorus you will be paid according to a stipulated pay scale. Negotiation is not possible.

◆ The addresses and names of the chorus masters can be found in the *Deutsches Bühnenjahrbuch*.

# 6

# The Singing Business

## The cultural system in Germany

In Germany, the Federal States are politically and financially responsible for education and culture (*die Kulturhoheit der Länder*). Opera houses, theatres, orchestras and cultural events in general are highly subsidized by the Federal States or the cities. Sponsorship does play a certain role but it will never replace the subsidy system in the near future.

## The opera houses

As a result of the present financial climate, some opera houses were forced to close down, whilst others have had to merge with other houses. In 2005 there were approximately 90 opera houses in the German-speaking countries (Germany, Austria and parts of Switzerland).

**The different opera houses**

There are three different kinds of opera houses in Germany:
* The City Opera House (*das Stadttheater*) financed by the city
* *Das Landestheater* similar to the City Opera House
* The State Opera House (*das Staatstheater* or *die Staatsoper*) financed by the Federal State

### A, B, C and D houses

In colloquial German we speak of *das Theater* to mean the physical building as well as the institution. The opera houses are divided into A, B, C and D houses. This classification refers to the size of the orchestra and determines the salaries of the orchestral players and chorus members. D houses are the smallest and A houses (mostly State Theatres) the biggest.

# 6 ♦ The Singing Business

It is important for a beginner to know that the quality of a house is not necessarily dependent on its classification. Sometimes a D house will prove to be just as good for starting a career as a C house. It is more important that there is an artistic director who will take care of the young singers and give them roles suitable to their vocal development.

## The contract

Most theatre contracts are based on the *Normalvertrag Bühne* (standard theatre contract), which is an agreement between the employer's association *Deutscher Bühnenverein* (German Theatre Association) and the *Genossenschaft Deutscher Bühnenangehöriger* (The Union of Theatre Employees). The present valid version dates from 15 October 2002.

Singers should read their contracts very carefully. They will contain paragraphs specifically concerning the singers' rights and obligations.

Your contract is valid only after it is countersigned by the theatre! Your signature alone has no validity!

**The different contracts**

There are in general two kinds of contracts:
* *Der Festvertrag*, permanent employment for at least one complete season
* *der Gastvertrag/Stückvertrag*, guest appearances in specified operas

The season runs for twelve months, starting from the middle of August and lasting until the end of June, followed by six weeks' vacation. One refers to it as the 2006/2007 season (*die Spielzeit 2006/2007*).

Once you have a signed permanent contract for one season you become a soloist in the theatre ensemble. You are engaged for the entire season and will receive a monthly salary (*das Monatsgehalt*). Taxes, health and social insurance will be subtracted automatically (PAYE) and the net amount (*netto*) will be paid into your current account (*das Girokonto*).

The other variant is the guest contract for a part of the season or a single production. In this case, you do not become an ensemble member, and under certain circumstances may get your entire fee without any subtractions (*brutto*). In this case, it is important to find out how much you will be taxed. We highly recommend that you put that sum aside immediately or you might get a very unpleasant surprise at the end of the financial year.

After all deductions, your net income should be more or less two-thirds of your gross (*brutto*) income. This amount differs depending on whether you are single, have children or are married.

**Renewing the contract**

Your one-year contract (*der Festvertrag*) will be renewed automatically for the following season unless the theatre (i. e. *der Intendant*) gives you official notice by 31 October. This has to be in writing and is called *die Nichtverlängerungs-Mitteilung*. Your employer is obliged to invite you to a hearing (*die Anhörung*) before this letter can be sent. Consult the spokesperson for the soloists (*der Solistensprecher/die Solistensprecherin*), a member of the staff council (*der Personalrat*) or a member of the *Genossenschaft Deutscher Bühnenangehöriger* (the union) about your rights.

Should you wish to terminate your contract you must also give notice by 31 October. In this case, there will be no hearing. If you want to leave in midseason you can only hope for goodwill (*die Kulanz*) on the side of the management.

## How to negotiate a contract

**Agency**

If you get your job through an agent you will not have to negotiate your salary or fee. The agency will do it for you. The agent gets a commission which can be up to 12% of your monthly fee for one year. Ask the agency about their terms. Usually the opera house pays one half of the commission. The state agency *ZBF* is the only one that receives no commission at all.

# 6 • The Singing Business

**Negotiating for yourself**

If you do have to negotiate for yourself, the following tips may be useful:

* Make enquiries beforehand about the cost of living (flat or apartment, food, public transport) and calculate your future expenses.
* If the theatre asks you about your salary expectations never mention a figure. Answer instead with the question: "What are you prepared to pay?"
* You can assume that the theatre will first offer you the minimum. From there you can try to negotiate upwards, using the cost of living as your argument. But be realistic. You won't get more than another 5 to 10%, at best.
* The absolute minimum monthly salary a theatre is required to pay is 1,550 Euro gross (§ 58,1 *Normalvertrag Bühne*).
* The maximum salary for a beginner was 2,000 Euros at time of writing. This, however, applies only to the bigger houses.
* Your salary is paid according to union wage negotiations.
* Your voice type (*das Fach*) such as *Sopran* or *Bariton* will be part of your contract. Of course you must discuss the roles you will be singing and try to avoid those unsuitable for your voice type. But you will not be able to force the theatre to stipulate roles in your contract. You must be prepared to sing certain roles that do not ordinarily belong to the standard repertoire for your voice type.

The opera season (*die Spielzeit*) is usually planned well ahead of time. In bigger houses this can be four or five years in advance and in smaller houses perhaps six or eight months.

**Tips**

* In German, one writes a four-figure sum with a full-stop (period) instead of a comma, e.g. 1.000 Euros. A sum with Euro and Cent will be written 1.550,50.
  This is important to remember when you write out your bank transactions or receipts. In unofficial correspondence, the full-stop can also be left away.
* A salary (*das Gehalt/die Gage*) is a regular monthly payment. A fee (*das Honorar*) is a one-off payment.

## Taxes

At the beginning of your engagement (and thereafter at the beginning of each calendar year) you will have to hand in your Tax Card (*die Lohnsteuerkarte*) to your employer. This you get from the municipality or district council (*die Gemeindeverwaltung*) where you live.

**Tax Card**

If you belong to the Roman Catholic, Protestant or Jewish religion you will also have to pay a "Church Tax" in Germany. The Church Tax varies between 8 and 9% of your total payable income tax. If you do not wish to pay this tax or do not belong to one of these denominations, you have to declare that you do not have any religious affiliations in Germany and are consequently *konfessionslos* or *ohne Konfession*.

**Church Tax**

Your employer enters your earnings onto your Tax Card. You will get this card back at the end of the year. This has to be included along with your tax declaration for the Department of Revenue (*das Finanzamt*). The first time you declare your taxes in Germany it might be a good idea to visit a tax consultant (*der Steuerberater/die Steuerberaterin*). Ask your colleagues to recommend a consultant experienced in declaring singers' taxes.

**Tax Declaration**

## Visa and work permits

Excerpt from: www.auswaertiges-amt.de, the official site of the Federal Foreign Office of Germany:
"Foreign nationals from states outside the European Economic Area (EEA) may as a rule only work in Germany if they have a work permit. Such foreign nationals who wish to enter Germany in order to commence work may, because of the 1973 ban on recruitment and current high unemployment levels, only be issued with work permits in exceptional cases.

Foreign nationals who are entitled to freedom of movement under EU law, the Agreement on the European Economic Area or under bilateral agreements do not require a work permit in Germany. Nationals of the following states are thus exempt: Austria, Belgium, Cyprus, Denmark, Finland, France, Greece, Great Britain, Iceland, Ireland, Italy, Liechtenstein, Luxembourg, Malta, the Netherlands, Norway, Portugal, Spain, Sweden and Switzerland. Nationals of the following countries continue to require work permits, notwithstanding their countries' accession to the EU on 1 May 2004, because of the transitional rules relating to freedom of movement: the Czech Republic, Estonia, Hungary, Latvia, Lithuania, Poland, Slovakia and Slovenia.

Under German foreigners' law, foreign nationals who want to work in Germany also need a visa or a residence permit.

EU, EEA and Swiss nationals may acquire the necessary residence permit after they have arrived in Germany, as may nationals of Australia, Canada, Israel, Japan, New Zealand and the United States of America.

Nationals of all other countries must apply for a visa from their local German mission (consulate) before coming to Germany."

For up-to-date information concerning your visa (*das Visum*), residence permit (*die Aufenthaltsgenehmigung*) and work permit (*die Arbeitserlaubnis*) you should consult the website of the Federal Foreign Office of Germany or ask at the German Consulate in your own country. The administration of the opera house might also help you.

After you have auditioned in Germany and been offered a contract, you will have to go back to your own country in order to apply for the necessary visa. Be sure that you have a valid contract signed by both parties. This procedure can take up to five months.

## Money and Bank account

Currency

The valid currency in Germany, Belgium, Greece, Spain, France, Ireland, Italy, Luxembourg, the Netherlands, Austria, Portugal and Finland is the Euro (€).

One Euro = 100 Cents (ct).

When you come to Germany you will have to open a current account (*das Girokonto*). You should compare carefully what each bank charges and what services are provided.

**Current Account, Bank Card, Credit Card**

In Germany it is still customary to pay in cash for small transactions. Your bank will however furnish you with a bank card (*die Bankkarte*), with which you are able to withdraw money from cash machines (*der Bankautomat*), call up your bank statements (*der Kontoauszug*) and use for other banking activities. With the bank card you can pay in supermarkets, department stores and restaurants as well as withdraw money from cash machines. With a credit card (*die Kreditkarte*) you can pay for bigger expenses. Credit cards are not always accepted in shops or restaurants in Germany.

## Insurance

As a soloist with a *Festvertrag* or *Gastvertrag* or as a member of the chorus you will have to subscribe to the national health insurance. If you earn a gross monthly salary of 3,900.00 Euros or less (at time of writing) it will automatically be a compulsory insurance (*die Pflichtversicherung*). Although the differences between the various types of insurance may not seem so important at first glance, you should compare the offers thoroughly. Ask the administration of the opera house, your colleagues or find an independent consultant.

**Health Insurance**

If you earn more than 3,900.00 Euros, you no longer have to take out the compulsory insurance. Because of the high health costs, it will be important to then join a private insurance scheme (*die private Krankenversicherung*) or to stay voluntarily in the compulsory insurance scheme.

You will also join the national pension scheme (*die Rentenversicherung*). At the present time, pension reform is being debated in Germany and the future pension scheme will probably be just basic care and each employee will have to make sure that he or she obtains additional insurance as well.

**National Pension Scheme**

**Additional Insurance**

There is, however, additional insurance for artistic personnel that is regulated by the *Versorgungsanstalt der Deutschen Bühnen VddB* and administered by the *Bayerische Versorgungskammer* in Munich. It is mandatory to take out this insurance when you are employed at a German opera house with a *Festvertrag* or *Gastvertrag*. This is automatically organized by the theatre. Should you become unemployed it is recommended that you continue paying the monthly premium voluntarily (*die freiwillige Weiterversicherung*) in order to stay in the insurance scheme. The premium can be reduced to a minimum if you cannot afford the entire sum. Find out about this in good time from the *Bayerische Versorgungskammer – Versorgungsanstalt der deutschen Bühnen, 81921 München*.

This insurance at the *VddB* might also be changed in the near future. You should therefore talk to a professional independent consultant about any further provision for your retirement.

## Additional insurance for your everyday life

◆ Personal liability insurance (*die private Haftpflichtversicherung*): This is highly recommended for everyone and covers the often extremely high costs of accidents you might cause in your free time (this does not apply to accidents you cause as a car driver). It covers physical injury as well as damage to foreign property you might inadvertently cause.

◆ Professional indemnity insurance (*die Berufshaftpflichtversicherung*): Your personal liability insurance does not cover the costs of damage caused by you on the way to and from work, as well as during rehearsals and performances. We therefore recommend a professional indemnity insurance.

◆ Household insurance (*die Hausratversicherung*): Covers damage caused by yourself in your own home.

**Tip**

Find an independent consultant who will compare the offers of the various insurance companies.

## Professional organizations

* *Genossenschaft deutscher Bühnen-Angehöriger (GDBA)*
This is the union for stage artists and associated professions that provides legal advice as well as (after an initial membership of six months) legal protection. The membership fee is 1% of your monthly gross salary. www.buehnengenossen schaft.de.

* *Gesellschaft zur Verwertung von Leistungsschutzrechten*
You should become a member of this copyright company. As soon as you have made your first remunerated CD, Radio- or TV-recording in Germany, you receive money back from the GVL, but only if you are already a member. Membership is free. www.gvl.de.

Ensure that your home office is in order and running efficiently:

Tip

* Programmes, photos, cuttings, press material, papers, correspondence, contracts and sheet music should be in organized files so that you can find them quickly when you need them.
* Look after your music scores! If you have to make notes, use a soft pencil.
* Use a calendar that is spread over the next two or three years because contracts are made far ahead of time in Germany.
* See that you have professional business cards with the address and telephone numbers where you can be reached.
* Your e-mail messages or business letters should be written as professionally as possible (in good German, of course).
* Answer every business call or e-mail, even if it is only to acknowledge that you have received it.

Apart from your artistic abilities, professionalism and good business sense are the most important factors for a successful career.

# 7

# Vocal Hygiene

The life of a modern singer has become very strenuous and presents enormous physical and mental challenges. Pollution and general noise levels have become significant health factors. Singers work irregular hours and are expected to perform under every imaginable circumstance. They have to be highly flexible and learn to adjust to climate, cuisine and sudden time changes while travelling from country to country. Allergies also play a big role. Add to this the stress of striving for perfection every minute of the day in rehearsal and performance and you have one much stressed singer.

## Nutrition and health

The general health rules also apply to singers, only more so. It is essential to eat enough fruit, fresh vegetables and whole food to keep the balance between alkaline and acid foods in your diet and to provide you daily with enough vitamins and minerals so that your immune system becomes your ally and not your enemy.

This must be done in a balanced and sensible way. We have known singers who do not trust their immune systems and are obsessed with germs. It is far more productive to concentrate on keeping your body in perfect working order by eating and living in a healthy way.

General rules

- It is better to eat fruit and vegetables than to take vitamin pills.
- It is better to go for a brisk walk in the fresh air than to use your home jogger.
- Smoking is bad for your whole system, especially your voice.

- Do not eat or drink anything ice-cold before singing. It is far better to have a cup of herbal tea or warm water (not too hot, though).
- Alcohol not only has a negative influence on your body and mental alertness but it also dries out the mucous membranes in your throat.
- Chocolate, milk or nuts can cause too much mucous.
- Red wine, black tea or olives can cause a dry mouth, and consequently dry vocal folds. Even sugar can have this effect.
- Sour foodstuffs like tomatoes or lemon juice can irritate the throat.
- Avoid food that causes flatulence or acidity. Reflux can irritate the membranes of the throat especially when you are lying down. Therefore avoid eating too much or too sweet before going to bed.
- Avoid food or drink that is either too hot or too cold. This can have an adverse effect on your blood circulation.
- In general, it is never a good idea to eat too much before a performance. This will hamper your breathing mechanism.

> Each singer should make a list of things that have a negative influence on his or her voice or reactions. If you know, for instance, that your mouth dries out when you drink red wine, this is obviously a thing to avoid the day before a performance.

**Weight**

"The opera is not over until the fat lady sings" is most definitely no longer valid!
You need only look at the singers of today, Renée Fleming, Angelika Kirchschlager, Anna Netrebko, Nina Stemme, Roberto Alagna or Ronaldo Villazon to see that none of them is fat. Not only do you have less energy and breath control if you are overweight, but you will have practically no chance of finding a singing job in Germany today. The directors of today expect physical credibility from their singer-actors. The only fat singers who still have a chance are the tenors. And then they really have to be good! By the way, the opposite is also true – anorexic singers are definitely a "no-go".

# 7 • Vocal Hygiene

## You and your body

**Physical activity**

As a singer you will not only use your musicality and imagination onstage, you also need to become a performing machine. You have to train the vocal muscles, especially those for breathing, but you will also have to become aware of the importance of mobilizing every other muscle in your body. As a singer-actor you will be using them to express your emotions on stage and it is essential that you feel comfortable in your own body. Therefore it is important to find a physical activity that you enjoy and can pursue two or three times a week. We recommend power-walking, swimming or bicycling. If you can't do this, you should at least go for a long, brisk walk or do keep-fit exercises every day preferably in the fresh air. A window-shopping amble in a city polluted with exhaust fumes does not count! Swimming is considered the ideal sport for a singer, because it trains the breathing muscles as well as keeping you generally fit. Bodybuilding is not ideal because it can sometimes make the breathing muscles inflexible.

**Posture**

The way you stand or move not only has a direct influence upon your singing, but can also influence the psyche. Try walking around with rounded shoulders, a sunken chest and head bent and you will very soon be in a "hang-dog" mood. Walking with a straight spine and an energetic step can make you feel like the "king of the world".

Bad singing technique can cause tension in the neck and shoulders, so before running to your orthopaedic surgeon, consider whether your problems appeared after starting your singing lessons. You should discuss this with your teacher!

Without the "noble posture" (Richard Miller, The Structure of Singing) you will not only have difficulty with the necessary breath support for singing but you will also have tension in your neck and shoulders, which is detrimental to the singing voice.

If you have a spine problem, or your general posture is bad, have it treated as soon as possible. Not only does it look bad onstage but it could cause irreparable vocal damage. Do not take painkillers, muscle relaxants or similar medication, because you will only be treating the symptoms instead of looking at the causes. Go to a good physiotherapist or osteopath. You can also do many things by yourself. The Alexander technique, yoga, qigong or the Feldenkrais method are particularly good for singers. These methods can improve your posture as well as help you find the mental, spiritual and physical energy centres in your body.

## Mental fitness

A singer who is not both mentally and emotionally strong cannot survive. The profession makes extreme demands upon the emotions. Imagine having to play and sing a Butterfly or a Medea every other night and having to kill your children or yourself on stage. This is not easy, and an unbalanced person could have a serious breakdown. The same applies to Otello or Peter Grimes.

On the other hand, singing beautiful music every day can also be a healing process.

> If you feel that you are not up to the demands of the singing profession because of lack of self-confidence or family problems, you should go to a psychoanalyst before going into the profession.

But do not make the mistake of imagining that the music will heal all your problems.

## Stage fright

We do not know of any singers who do not suffer from a certain amount of stage fright. This can be very healthy and give you the necessary "edge" or "kick" to be exciting on stage. Most singers have learned to handle the "butterfly-in-the-tummy" feeling and usually forget about it once they immerse themselves in the role. But sometime stage fright cannot be overcome, and it then becomes a real threat to your performance. Your knees tremble, your throat is dry, your hands are wet, your pulse races and worst of all you can't find the deep breath support that you need so desperately. The main reason for being nervous is fear. You could be afraid of not singing well, of forgetting the words or of generally making a fool of yourself. This can be remedied. Analyze your singing – why are you afraid of the high note? Maybe you should talk to another voice expert apart from your singing teacher and find a way of improving your technique. Why are you afraid of forgetting your words? Maybe you should find another way of learning. You could shift your attention from "learning mere words" to "what is the story I'm telling". If you put the emphasis on the deeper meaning of your text, you will find that you are concentrating so much on the fascinating story you are telling that it will be impossible to forget the words. And you will also find that it is not all that terrible if you forget some words as long as you stay in character. The same goes for forgetting the notes. If you shift your attention to the deeper meaning of the music, you will automatically sing it correctly. There are some singers who count like mad. They stand on stage with a glazed look on their faces and count 35 bars to their next entrance. And then there are the singers who listen to the inner rhythms and harmonies of the music and know instinctively when they have to sing. The latter method is infinitely better.

If you suffer from stage fright that paralyzes you in performance and you find that you cannot control these symptoms, you should get professional help. Ask your doctor to give you the name of a psychologist who specializes in overcoming fear and anxiety. Under no circumstances should you take psycho-pharmaceutical drugs without the accompanying therapy. This is no solution and can only have a negative influence on your behaviour and on your voice production.

**The psycho-somatic trap**

Many inexperienced singers fall into the so-called "psycho-somatic trap". It is a particularly complicated form of stage fright. Have you noticed that you sometimes get a sore throat or laryngitis a day or two before having to sing something particularly important, like an audition or an opening night? Have you noticed that when you are having a relaxing holiday you can walk in the cold wind without a scarf and never once get sick? The next time you develop a cold before an important audition, it might be a good idea to sit down in your favourite meditation armchair and think about the situation. How often do I get sick? Under which circumstances do I get sick? Could it be that there is an underlying, psychological reason for my cold? Could it be that I am afraid to go onstage and am denying it? Could the sore throat just be a manifestation of fear? The problem with the psychosomatic trap is that if unchecked, it can get worse every time and become a very welcome and comfortable habit – "if I'm genuinely sick then I don't have to admit to my fear and I have a good reason for cancelling". Think about it. Maybe it's time to talk to your subconscious and give it a piece of your mind!

The fact that your sickness might have a psychological cause does not mean that you are not genuinely ill and should not go to the doctor for treatment.

## Pollution

We live in a very polluted environment. We are surrounded by noise and air pollution, which weakens our immune system every minute of the day.

Singers especially should see to it that they live in areas where this can be avoided as far as possible. Try if possible not to live in an area full of noise and exhaust fumes. Try to avoid inhaling cigarette smoke. Do not spend too much time with heavy smokers. Still, it is astonishing how much smoking goes on in theatres, in spite of the "No Smoking" signs and the obvious health risks. It goes without saying that a singer should not smoke because this can harm the vocal folds. Not only does inhaling smoke dry out the mucous membranes of the throat, but it can also cause permanent damage like Reinke's oedema or hyper plastic laryngitis. This could result in chronic, irreversible hoarseness.

**Smoking**

## The speaking voice

The way singers speak can influence their singing voice. Speaking too much or too loudly, without the correct breath support causes tension in the throat and can even cause hoarseness. The same applies to singers who speak in a lower or higher range than their natural speaking voice. It goes without saying that you should under no circumstances go to loud parties or bars on the evening before a performance because you will have to shout to be heard, apart from being exposed to cigarette smoke. Very few singers have vocal folds that are strong enough to stand that kind of abuse.

**Tip**

◆ On the day of a performance we suggest that you do your first set of voice-warming exercises as soon as you get up, because this will ensure that you will speak with breath support for the rest of the day (see chapter 8).
◆ Singers often have to speak dialogue on stage. The same rules apply for speaking onstage as for singing onstage. Never speak stage dialogue without warming up the voice and without using adequate breath support.

## Dryness

Why does one always see singers before auditions and at rehearsals carting bottles of water around? They are all terrified that this gremlin will rear its ugly head. Dryness makes our voices feel gritty and inflexible, and singing on a dry throat causes vocal irritation and hoarseness.

**Causes for a dry throat**

◆ Dusty, overheated and airless rooms
◆ Cigarette smoke
◆ Certain foodstuffs (see "nutrition")
◆ Decongestant medication taken for a cold
◆ Stage fright
◆ Dehydration from not drinking enough water

- Train and air journeys
- Some antihistamines could cause dryness. Take them with plenty of water

- Drink at least two litres (eight glasses) of water per day. If you have a cold you should increase it to three litres (twelve glasses) a day.
- Air your apartment regularly and remove dust-catchers like carpets and heavy curtains.
- Use a humidifier. Don't buy a cheap one. Ask your doctor to recommend the best one for your purposes.
- When you are travelling (especially flying) see to it that you drink enough water. No coffee or soda pop, and definitely no alcohol. These beverages will only cause more dryness! Drink at least half a litre (two glasses) of water per hour whilst travelling. Additionally, you could use an isotonic humidifying spray for your mouth and nose.

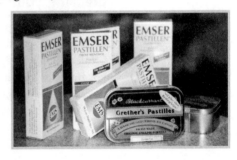

- Ask your pharmacist to recommend soothing throat lozenges (without sugar).
- For dryness before a performance, we recommend drinking warm water or peppermint tea.

If your mouth becomes dry on stage you could try visualizing a slice of lemon. Imagine biting into the lemon and sucking out the sour-tasting juices. You will be surprised how much saliva you will suddenly have in your mouth!

## Vocal trauma

You can cause damage to your vocal folds by lifting heavy weights. Next time your pianist asks you to help him shift the piano, try to breathe lightly through your throat without pressing the vocal folds together.

# 7 • Vocal Hygiene

We know of a singer who lost her voice completely after moving house. She did not realize that she grunted like a weight lifter every time she lifted a box.

## Sex

Despite all rumours to the contrary, it is not damaging to the voice to have sex on the day before a performance! It is a different matter though, if you tend to scream or moan during this pleasant pastime. Find a way to enjoy without vocalizing!

## Clearing your throat

"One of the most prevalent forms of vocal abuse is incessant, habitual, non-productive throat clearing" (Joseph C. Stemple, Clinical Voice Pathology). Should you notice that you have got into this bad habit, you should stop immediately. If you have a cold and have to get rid of mucous, try to do this by swallowing hard or coughing lightly.

## The voice specialist

If you have a persistent voice problem which will not go away, you should consult a good laryngologist or voice specialist (der Phoniater). A normal ear-nose-and-throat specialist does not necessarily have the specialized knowledge that a singer needs. If you notice that your voice becomes tired quickly, or you have difficulty swallowing, visit a specialist who works extensively with singers. You could have a chronic infection or a condition caused by vocal abuse. If you are near a university with a voice clinic, this would be the place to go, providing they have somebody specializing in the singing voice.

If you notice that your voice becomes hoarse or tired after your singing lesson, it is very possible that you are using the wrong technique. This should be remedied immediately; even if it means having to tell a teacher you adore that something is very wrong. Vocal tiredness or hoarseness can also be caused by singing a role which is too heavy or too difficult for you. Maybe you should rather leave Rigoletto until later and concentrate right now on Guglielmo?

> If you know that you have a strenuous role to sing, start preparing for it vocally very early. Once you start stage rehearsals, there will be no time to think of careful singing. The technical difficulties have to be solved beforehand.

## The immune system

When you are healthy, your immune system protects you against bacterial or viral infections. But your immune system will let you down if you do not look after it.

*Antibiotics*

Mental and physical stress, pollution or wrong eating habits can cause your immune system to fail. Taking antibiotics may cure you on a short-term basis, but taken regularly they will weaken your natural resistance against infection.

There are many other ways to clear up or prevent infections:
- Eat fresh vegetables, fruit and full-grain products
- Avoid junk food
- Drink enough water, fresh fruit juices and herbal teas, without sugar
- Pursue regular sport activities in the fresh air
- Get enough sleep
- Learn stress-management
- Use natural medicines, such as vitamin C, zinc, echinacea, sage or thyme to cure an infection
- Wear appropriate clothing. Being too warmly dressed can be just as damaging as wearing too little

There are singers who take a tremendous amount of chemically produced vitamin products without actually knowing that this also can have an adverse affect on their health. If taken in overdose, some vitamins can ruin your health. Read

*Tip*

up about this and find out exactly which ingredients are in the product you are taking before you pour everything into your system. A healthy person normally does not need additional vitamin supplements.

## You and your doctor

You should only go to doctors whom you trust implicitly. Your house doctor should be aware of the fact that as a singer your throat and breathing mechanism are especially sensitive. On the other hand, you cannot always expect your general practitioner to understand exactly what your specific needs are. In Germany, *der Beipackzettel* (an instruction sheet describing contents, dosage and possible side effects) is included in every packet of medication. You should read this carefully. Under no circumstances should you take medication without finding out exactly how it might affect your voice.

## Anaesthesia

Intubation

If you have to undergo an operation, you should have a long talk with your anaesthetist beforehand. Try to avoid intratracheal intubation, which is the usual method used when giving a general anaesthetic. If this is not possible, you should request a thinner tube that will not damage the vocal folds. Any operation in the region of the throat should be most carefully considered. Because of the anatomical relationships of the thyroid, heart, lungs and carotid arteries to the laryngeal and vagus nerves (which supply your larynx), surgical procedures by an inexperienced surgeon involving these structures could damage the nerves leading to the larynx. Possible consequences may be vocal fold paralysis or a loss of sensory perception in the mucosal lining of the larynx. If possible, ask for a second opinion before considering an operation.

## Nodules and contact ulcers

Vocal nodules are a direct result of chronic vocal abuse and occur mostly in children and female adults. Male singers who abuse their voices usually develop a contact ulcer, which then develops into a granuloma if not treated. The treatment of vocal nodules or contact ulcers should always include voice therapy. Occasionally, growths on the vocal folds may require surgical removal. This is the case when the nodules or the granuloma have been present for a long time and have grown hard and fibrous. Should your voice doctor recommend an operation, you should ask him if there is any alternative treatment for your disorder. In 90% of the cases, you can be successfully treated by appropriate voice therapy. A good voice therapist will be able to analyze exactly what you have been doing wrong. Under no circumstances should you rush into an operation before consulting a specialized therapist. The therapist will focus on vocal hygiene, the training of healthy vocal habits and will counsel you on the causes of the pathology. He might recommend anything from resting the voice for a few weeks to changing your singing technique or your teacher.

Voice therapy

The vocal folds can also be damaged by the following:
* chronic bronchitis (causing coughing and throat clearing)
* chronic laryngitis
* mucous drainage caused by allergies or sinus conditions
* smoking
* excessive use of alcohol
* stomach disorders such as increased acidity with accompanying reflux.

Vocal damage

The symptoms can be a "tired voice", pain during swallowing, hoarseness, total loss of voice or even nodules and granulomas.

## The theatre doctor

Once you are in the business, you might find that the theatre doctor, who happens to be on duty during a performance, could turn out to be a retired gynaecologist who loves opera! If you are in vocal trouble or even lose your voice during a performance, this doctor will come to your dressing room and probably recommend a calcium injection or a high dosage of cortisone. This might save the performance, but could have an adverse effect on your health in the long run. It is not a good idea to sing on inflamed vocal folds, even if you feel so much better because of the cortisone (see further down). It is also not a good idea to have an injection of calcium in a high dosage without having an ECG beforehand. We suggest that you discuss this problem with your voice specialist or laryngologist, so that you know what to do in case of an emergency.

## When to cancel

The singer's instinct

A singer is often faced with the problem of having to decide whether to sing a performance (or rehearsal) while sick. This is where your greatest ally, "the singer's instinct", comes into the picture. You have the first symptoms of an infection, you are in the last week of rehearsals before an important performance and you drag yourself to the rehearsals because you don't want to let your colleagues down. Is that clever? Might it not be better to stay in bed for two days, look after yourself and then sing the opening night as a healthy singer? You certainly do not help your colleagues by coming to rehearsals sick and spraying your germs all over the place!

The first thing to do is to go to your laryngologist. If your vocal folds are infected and swollen, you must cancel, even if it is the opening night. Do not allow the *Intendant*, conductor or stage director to put you under pressure. You are the only one who knows what your voice can do and you must stand firm.

120

On the other hand, you should know your voice so well that you are able to judge exactly how it will behave. When you get up in the morning and try out your voice, don't panic if it does not function. Have a hot shower and a good breakfast, do your physical exercises and then start doing some very careful breathing and vocal exercises. In most cases, the voice will come back and will get you through the evening!

If your doctor diagnoses a laryngeal infection he will tell you not to sing or talk for a few days. This also goes for whispering! It is just as damaging for the voice to whisper as it is to shout. If you have to communicate, then rather talk with a full, supported voice – only softly.

**Tip**

## Allergies

Allergies belong to the so-called "diseases of the 20th and 21st century". We are surrounded by pollutants, which weaken our immune systems and make us susceptible to infections and allergies. Have them treated as soon as possible and try to avoid getting into contact with allergens.

**Asthma and hay fever**

Allergic asthma and hay fever should not prove an insurmountable problem for a singer. We know of at least three world-famous singers who are asthma or hay fever sufferers. You should however be very careful about choosing the right treatment.
* If you have to use a spray, it should be an inhalator without a chemical propellant, because you might be allergic to the propellant.
* Sprays could cause hoarseness after many years of use. It helps to use a spacer for administering the spray.
* If you take antihistamines, avoid them before a performance as they can make you very tired and dry out your voice.

## Medical hazards

**Beware of**

◆ Aspirin or any other medication containing acetylsalicylic acid. Aspirin is often prescribed to prevent cardiovascular complaints because it thins the blood, but it is exactly this property that can cause haemorrhaging of the vocal folds during heavy singing. If you only need a painkiller, we suggest that you use products containing paracetamol rather than acetylsalicylic acid.

◆ Throat lozenges containing benzocaine, lidocaine, tetracaine or dequalinium. These will anaesthetize your throat and as a result reduce the sensory feedback while singing.

◆ Tablets or nasal sprays that contain decongestants because they dry out the mucous membranes of the larynx.

◆ Anabolic steroids because they influence your hormones and thus also the voice.

◆ Beta-blockers, some medications for high blood pressure and certain psycho-pharmaceutical products can also be detrimental to the voice. Ask your doctor.

### Cortisone

Cortisone is a very seductive drug. On the one hand it is one of the wonder-drugs of the 20th century and sometimes absolutely essential for the treatment of infections and allergies. On the other hand, it makes the singing process feel so easy that a singer should beware of using it too often. Cortisone (corticosteroids) may mask the signs of infection and new infections may appear during their use, without being detected. Prolonged or regular use of corticosteroids could (in rare cases) cause high blood pressure, muscle weakness, hoarseness, yeast or fungal infections of nose or throat (thrush) as well as cataracts.

## The female voice

Women often have to take hormones for different reasons.
A female singer should be aware of the special problems that
could arise from this. If you have to take hormonal medication (i.e. as a contraceptive), ask your doctor to tell you
whether they contain testosterone or progesterone, which
might change your voice production. Another factor that
could influence the female voice is the swelling of the vocal
folds, which is a pre-menstrual symptom. Women who are
affected in this way should try to sing very carefully during
these few days.

Good singers always take responsibility for their physical and
mental health. They follow their instincts and listen carefully
to their body and psyche. They know their needs and can
look after themselves most of the time.

# 8

# The Principles of Good Singing

In this chapter, we will try to explain as simply as possible what we think you should know in order to make your voice flexible and long lasting. We are aware of the fact that one cannot learn singing from a book. Nevertheless, we would like to put a few basic ideas forward that have been used for many years by many good singers.

"The good singer must put his whole soul into the interpretation of a passage if it is not to appear wooden and stilted. This facility is dependent upon a complete mastery of technique and the control, not merely of the mechanics of singing, but the fine shades of tone colour which defy analysis but convey the emotional message of a passage … For the singer, good anatomical endowment is essential, though it is not in itself enough. Beautiful singing needs seven or more years of arduous practice in the acquisition of the requisite techniques before the art emerges and the soul is liberated from the bonds of constant striving" (Margaret Greene, The Voice and its Disorders).

A good singing voice should include following qualities:

**Qualities of a good singing voice**

* Beauty of tone
* Flexibility
* Complete control of the instrument
* Carrying power
* Clear diction
* Pure intonation
* Style and musicality (*die Gesangskultur*)
* A recognizable and characteristic timbre
* Focus and presence
* Longevity
* Emotional power

# Vocal Faults

It is generally recognized that the following factors are not acceptable:

* A singing sound without the natural vibrato (*die Schwingung*) that characterizes the individual voice. The voice sounds too dark or too "white"
* A "spread" sound that sounds shrill and ugly
* A forced harsh sound that sounds more like screaming than singing
* An inability to sing piano
* A quick vibrato, also called tremolo or *caprino* (little goat)
* A slow vibrato, also called a "wobble"
* A powerless tone without breath support
* Impure intonation. The tone is either too high or too low
* A nasal sound
* A throaty sound (*der Knödel*)
* A dark muffled sound (*abgedunkelt*)
* A chronic hoarse sound
* The larynx suddenly jumps up when the voice changes register (*der Kickser*)
* A breathy sound
* Superfluous movements of facial muscles such as exaggerated lip movements, a trembling jaw, mouth pulled to one side or other facial grimaces
* Bad posture such as raised shoulders, tension in the arms and hands, locked knees, head pulled back or lower jaw pushed forward
* A stiff upper lip. You might need this in other situations but not when you're singing!

**Vocal faults**

## The singing teacher

"The whole object of learning to sing is to improve the connection between the emotional, poetic, and musical impulses and the body which responds by producing appropriate sound. It is a process demanding patience and total dedication, in which a good teacher can be of the greatest

125

help and the wrong teacher can do untold damage. It is a process in which the initiative must always be taken by singers themselves ... The study of singing ... can be reduced to two things:

♦ Training the mind and the imagination to give clear and precise impulses to which the body can react.

♦ Training the body to react with maximum precision and energy" (Thomas Hemsley, Singing and Imagination).

**Take responsibility for your voice** — The first step should be to find a singing teacher who can help you achieve these goals. But that will not be enough! You should also listen to good singers, read what they have to say about their methods and then try things out for yourself. Listen very carefully and objectively to recordings of your own voice. You are responsible for your own voice and there is no such thing as "my teacher ruined my voice". You should use your intelligence and instincts to verify your technical development from the very first lesson onwards. If you feel that you are straining your voice during the lesson or that you have pains in your throat, or your voice is hoarse after a lesson, you should under no circumstances ignore the signs but ask a professional for his or her opinion.

It is easier for a newborn turtle to reach the ocean without being eaten than it is to find a good singing teacher.

Change your teacher if necessary. If you find that you can sing the highest and lowest notes without a problem and that your voice production feels free and easy, then you and your teacher are doing the right things.

## A good singing teacher

♦ has patience
♦ has a diagnostic ear
♦ has a good knowledge of the anatomical and physiological functions of the vocal instrument
♦ has a good knowledge of the vocal repertoire
♦ can explain the function of the voice in understandable terms
♦ recognizes the importance of efficient breath management

126

- recognizes the importance of singing piano and does not allow you to sing too loudly or to force your voice
- starts developing your voice from the middle register
- never allows you to sing arias that are too difficult but uses *arie antiche* or other easy songs to start with
- is flexible and can adjust the exercises to your individual needs
- understands the psychological problems affecting the singing process
- keeps a friendly but professional distance
- understands that singing technique is only the beginning of the art of singing

### A teacher who might harm you
- will tell you to lie on the floor and put bricks on your stomach
- lets you sing with a cork in your mouth
- manipulates your larynx or presses down your tongue with a spatula
- wants you to sing advanced arias from the beginning before you have learnt breath management
- makes you sing *forte* all the time
- cannot explain adequately how breath support works
- causes you to use exaggerated facial grimaces and other bodily contortions to find the placement of your voice
- allows you to sing arias before your voice is "warmed up"
- concentrates only on technique and says nothing about interpretation
- criticizes you all the time and gives no positive feedback
- invades and controls your private life

If you feel that you do not understand or have difficulty executing what your teacher is telling you to do, you should do something about it. The first step would be to discuss it honestly with your teacher. This might clear up things you may not understand. You might be doing your exercises incorrectly when practicing at home. Secondly, you could try to solve the

**What to do if your teacher is not helping but harming you**

problem by listening differently. If the teacher is an excellent singer whose voice you admire, the problem might be that he is not very good at explaining. It might be better to listen to the way he sings and then try to copy it.

**When to stop working with a singing teacher**

If nothing helps and you still feel tension or pain in your throat or are hoarse after a lesson, then you should immediately discontinue working with this teacher. This can be very difficult and unpleasant for a young singer, because some teachers do not take kindly to rejection. Remember, it is your voice and your artistic future that is at stake!

Birgit Nilsson, one of the greatest dramatic sopranos of all time, went to the Stockholm Conservatoire as a young singer and discovered after a year of suffering that her teacher was harming her voice. She then discontinued her studies with him. "Instead of intensifying the tone in the frontal resonance chambers by using a more slender tone production, he put the entire burden directly on the vocal chords. This created an enormous tension in the throat. While it is true that with this method the tone became more intense, the tone sat in the wrong place and was entirely without overtones. He knew nothing about the principle of deep breathing, where the tone rests gently on the air column. Only thus can the tone be placed correctly and the vocal chords be free to do their incredibly difficult work" (Birgit Nilsson, La Nilsson. Mein Leben für die Oper).

**Finding the right teacher**

It is very difficult to find the right teacher. You could ask student colleagues who sing well with whom they study. You could work with a good coach who might be able to help you define your exact vocal problems and then recommend a teacher. Or you could go to the stage door of your nearest opera house and ask an established singer (whom you admire) whether he has time to listen to you and give you some advice. You could also read about singing methods and test the techniques by listening intelligently and objectively to a recording of your own efforts, but this can be dangerous without help from an objective professional.

If you do not find a teacher immediately, it is essential that you at least work with a top-class coach who has a good ear. These you will find in the bigger opera houses.

## The correct singing technique

There are as many techniques as there are singers in the world. When you listen to professional singers, you will hear throaty altos, darkened basses, shrill sopranos and nasal tenors, but there are just as many singers with beautiful, resonant and healthy voices who sing until a very advanced age. What is their secret?

After listening to and talking to many of these great singers, we have come to the conclusion that there are some universal rules that guarantee beauty of tone, flexibility, carrying power and a long-lasting voice that withstands the rigors of time.

## Hearing the sound first

"Beautiful sounds start in the mind of the singer. If you cannot think a beautiful sound it is an accident if you make one ... The best way to achieve the proper mental image of beautiful vocal sound is by listening intelligently to a sizable number of artist singers ... The important thing is to arrive at a vocal model which can serve as a guide and goal in your own pursuit of vocal excellence" (James C. McKinney, The Diagnosis and Correction of Vocal Faults).

The sound-producing muscles, the vocal folds (also called vocal chords), cannot be voluntarily controlled as you would control lifting an arm. The folds vibrate

Some singers think that they can "put" the voice into the mask by pulling up the corners of the mouth and pushing the cheek muscles up. Our opinion is that this could cause tension in the muscles leading to the larynx, thereby lifting the larynx into a position which is too high for the open and free voice. It also looks very unnatural and cannot be conveyed into your singing performance.

automatically as the air streams from the lungs. There is also no way that you can "throw" the sound into the "mask resonance" by using muscle control. These actions can only be produced by listening to good singing and then imagining the sound before you start to sing.

Not only should you listen to good singers but you should also observe good singers. What are they doing with their bodies? What are they doing with their mouths and their lips? You might find that singers who have an oval and relaxed mouth generally make a more beautiful tone than singers who "spread" their lips in a grimace or open their mouths too wide.

**Listening and feeling**

After learning to listen to other singers, it is important that you know how to "listen" to your own voice. This should be more of a kinaesthetic "feeling" than that of a "listening". Everybody knows that the voice sounds different from the inside of one's own head and that you cannot form an objective opinion of your own sound unless you listen to a recording of your voice. The secret is to "imagine" the good sound before singing. This will prepare the sound-producing muscles. When you produce a tone and your teacher or coach says that it sounds good, you should "feel" the sensation and use this feeling next time you want the same effect.

## Breath support or management

**Muscular control**

"Breath management is the institution of volitional muscular control over the respiratory function whose design and purpose it is to steady the tone and regulate breath expenditure" (Cornelius Reid, A Dictionary of Vocal Terminology).

Power, flexibility and perfect voice control are only possible if you understand how to use the breathing muscles to support the voice in such a way that the voice feels free and the throat is relaxed. Most singing faults like breathiness, lack of power, forced high notes, a tight throat, lack of flexi-

130

bility and the inability to sing *piano*, are caused by ineffective breath support. Every good singer should be able to produce a perfect *messa di voce* (starting on a *piano*, swelling the tone to a *forte* and coming back to the *piano* with perfect control) throughout the whole vocal range. This is only possible with efficient breath support, also called "breath management".

**Diaphragm**

It is a misconception that the diaphragm can be controlled voluntarily to play a role in breath management. You can find this out yourself by doing the following exercise:
Stand with your back to a wall and place your feet 6 inches (about 15 centimetres) from the wall. Now come up in a straight position (don't stick out your behind) without using your hands to push off. Observe which muscles you use for this action. An experienced singer will find that all the muscles of the torso (the back, the flanks and the stomach) are being used. Now stand in a natural position and voluntarily contract these same muscles without breathing in or out. You will find that you can do this quite easily. These are the muscles that you should be using for your breath support. Now stand easy and visualize your diaphragm as a large muscle that is attached to the back, front and sides of the torso and lies like a big flat rubber plate between the respiratory system and the digestive system. Now, without breathing, try to move this muscle up and down. You will find that you are moving other muscles but most definitely not the diaphragm. This proves that you cannot consciously and voluntarily use the diaphragm to control your breathing.

> "The feeling of being well grounded ... has nothing to do with an exaggerated tightening and holding of the muscles around the midriff – that energy blockage which is a sure way of denying to the breathing apparatus the freedom it needs for efficient, strong and flexible activity" (Thomas Hemsley, Singing and Imagination).

**Training of the breathing muscles**

The intercostals (*die Zwischenrippenmuskeln*, pl) and the muscles of the torso (*der Rumpf*) are the main muscle groups responsible for the singer's breath management. They are found in the chest, flanks, back, stomach and lower abdomen. Ideally, a singer should use all of these muscles while singing, but each singer should find a way that is most efficient for him or her. Some high sopranos prefer to use the upper chest and back muscles more than the other muscles. The powerful tenors and basses might prefer the lower abdominals. Many singers find that mainly using their flank muscles suffices. The young singer should find out by trial and error which muscle groups to use, but should understand one very important fact: The breathing muscles have to be trained in the same way that an athlete trains his muscles for running a marathon. It is not enough to use your normal breathing mechanism. Breath management for singing is very specific and has to be trained for many years before the ideal voice support is achieved. At the end of this chapter we will recommend a few exercises for strengthening the breathing muscles.

"The best way to gain control of the exhalation process is to try to maintain the expansion around the middle of the body – in the upper abdomen, the lower ribs and the back – while the diaphragm slowly begins to release its tension ... By a process of trial and error ... the singer learns to adjust this balanced tension just enough to supply the needed breath pressure for a given pitch and dynamic level ... Only time and disciplined practice will bring the support mechanism to its full potential for supplying fine adjustments of breath pressure to the vocal chords" (James C. McKinney, The Diagnosis and Correction of Vocal Faults).

This expansion of the body is also called *appoggio*, which comes from the Italian verb *appogiare* meaning to lean, to lean against, to support, and to sustain. This feeling of leaning against or expanding is a conscious muscular effort. During singing, your body should feel alert and buoyant. You should have a feeling as if your breathing column is a strong fountain and the voice is a ping-pong ball gently floating up and down on top of this force.

"Relaxation is the most abused word in singing studios today. Expressions such as poise, alertness, tonicity, buoyancy are more appropriate and accurate" (Thomas Hemsley, Singing and Imagination).

During the singing process, you should stand or sit in a relaxed and poised manner, with relaxed shoulders, neck and throat and be fully aware that the actual work is being done by the intercostals and other muscles of the torso. Always observe the "noble posture" (Richard Miller, The Structure of Singing). Observe yourself in the mirror. If you find that you are lifting up your shoulders or going up on your toes before or during the phrase, this means that you are using the shoulders or legs as your voice-supporting muscles, which is inefficient.

It is important to understand that breath management does not necessarily mean taking a huge amount of breath. "It is a misconception that the ability to sing long phrases is in direct relationship to the quantity of air you can inhale ... the ability to sing long phrases comes primarily from the efficiency of your vocal chord action ... The best corrective procedure for a breathy sound is to train the vocal chords to close properly, thereby eliminating or minimizing the excess breath ... The thought of beginning a humming sound will bring the vocal chords together and close the glottis" (James C. McKinney, The Diagnosis and Correction of Vocal Faults).

"A deep, full breath with the lungs filled to capacity, produces a feeling of fullness and stiffness which is not suitable for singing. The great Battistini went so far as to say that the longer the phrase he had to sing, the less breath he took, and never more than necessary to sniff the perfume of a tiny flower" (Thomas Hemsley, Singing and Imagination).

## The open throat

A letter dated April 4, 1944 from Birgit Nilsson to her mentor Ragnar Blennow explains it exactly: "I've just found the answer, and believe me it really makes a difference – everything sounds so full and round now ... One morning I woke up and was thinking about what I should do. Your words were still ringing in my ears that I should *open up all the way*. I jumped out of bed and relaxed my throat and let the air simply stream through. What a difference! I couldn't believe my ears. In the past I had tightened my throat and squeezed out the air, so that the sound became sharp and strained" (Birgit Nilsson, La Nilsson. Mein Leben für die Oper).

**The beginning of the yawn**

The free open throat or pharynx (*der weite Rachenraum*) is one of the most important factors in singing. Not only does it enhance the beauty of the voice but it also frees the sound, thus enabling it to "fly" into the mask resonance (*der schlanke Sitz*).

"By virtue of its position, size, and degree of adjustability, the pharynx (throat) has to qualify as the most important resonator ... Because of its size, the pharynx is capable of bringing out the lower partials of the vocal tone when it is properly used. The resulting quality is described by terms such as fullness, roundness, warmth, richness, or mellowness ... The ideal way to arrive at a proper concept of the 'open' throat is by learning to maintain the beginning-of-the-yawn position. Analyze the beginning of a yawn carefully and you will find that it can accomplish all of the following. It
* opens the pathway for a noiseless and almost effortless taking in of air,
* positions the larynx in a comfortably low position without tensing to do so,
* increases the size of the throat, especially in the vertical dimension, by lowering the larynx, gently lifting the soft palate, and relaxing the constrictor muscles of the pharynx wall.
* relaxes the muscles controlling the articulators, thus freeing them for action.
There are few situations where a singer can get so many beneficial results with so little expenditure of effort" (James C. McKinney, The Diagnosis and Correction of Vocal Faults).

It is important to use the beginning of the yawn because once you have reached the end of the yawn the throat is already closing and the larynx will rise up again, which is not what you want.

Singers who do not understand the importance of the open throat position make sounds that are "spread" and "screechy". They also have difficulty changing registers and often have a *Kickser* (the larynx suddenly jumping up during an ascending phrase). A tight throat (with the resulting high larynx position) also causes the quick vibrato or tremolo known as *caprino* (the little goat). Singers who use the open throat throughout the singing phrase from bottom to top will find that they do not have to think too much about changing registers and their voices feel "free" in all ranges.

Most singing teachers are aware of the importance of maintaining a "low larynx" at all times. This enables the singer to sing the highest as well as the lowest notes effortlessly (providing the breath management is efficient). The only problem is that some teachers tell the pupil to "push down" the larynx. This is practically as impossible as pushing down the diaphragm. It would be far easier to say, "lift up your soft palate and relax your jaw" as in the beginning of the yawn, because this automatically enables the larynx to maintain its naturally low position.

**Tip**

For the beginning-of-the-yawn position and the resultant lifting of the soft palate (*das Gaumensegel*) you should establish that your jaw is always in a relaxed and lowered position at the joint. This does not mean that the mouth is opened wide. The opposite should be the case.

**Vowels**

When we talk about vowels, we always mean the phonetic pronunciation, i. e.:

*a* as in the Italian *mare*
*e* as in the Italian *vero*
*i* as in the German *Liebe*
*o* as in the Italian *core*
*u* as in the German *Ruhe*
*ö* as in the German *böse*
*ü* as in the German *müde*

### Vowel modulation

To maintain the feeling of an open throat during singing, it is essential to understand the practice of vowel modulation (*der Vokalausgleich*). This means mixing the open Italian *a* or *o* into the other vowels while still keeping the purity of the original vowel. In actual fact, what happens is that the space in the back of the throat is opened wider than normal when speaking. When you observe good singers carefully, you will notice that they modulate the vowels so subtly that only an expert will notice, and this is why the voice sounds rounder and fuller. They mostly also use an oval mouth position.

**Example 1**

The difficult phrase on "Konstanze" that Belmonte sings in the fifth scene of *Die Entführung aus dem Serail*:

The first vowel should be an open Italian *o* (with a big space in the back of the throat) to bring it into the same placement as the next vowel which is an open *a*.

To maintain the same beauty of tone now established on the first two vowels, one must pronounce the *e* in the last vowel, as in "nurse", which can be done by relaxing the jaw and using an open *ö* without pursing the lips. The original *e* vowel will still be understood by the audience.

**Example 2**

The first phrase of Tamino's aria, "Dies Bildnis ist bezaubernd schön":

The *i* in "Dies" should be slightly mixed with an *ü*. Because the "Bildnis" lies high, both *i* vowels should be even more mixed with *ü* to open the back of the throat while still keeping the tongue in a relatively high position to ensure that the vowel is still understood. This prevents a *Kickser* and a sharp, ugly tone. The "ist" is again slightly mixed with an *ü*. The "be-" of "bezaubernd" is mixed with an *ö* (like in "nurse") and the "zau-" should start on a lovely open Italian *a*, coming down on the *u* at the very last moment. The "-bernd" is again mixed with *ö*. This ensures that the quality and beauty of tone stays the same on every note.

The last few phrases of Pamina's aria in *Die Zauberflöte*:

The first phrase, "so wird Ruh", is very difficult because the "Ruh" goes up onto a high note. Every high note needs space in the back of the throat and consequently the vowel modulation is all the more important there. The space in the back of the throat should be prepared during the two notes preceding the high note.

The vowel in "so" is an open Italian *o* and the *i* in "wird" is mixed with an *ü*, thereby creating an equality of tone in the two vowels. The "Ruh" should be nearly an *o* to produce a perfect sound. It is then easy to come back on the next phrase, "im Tode sein". The "im" is mixed with *ü*. The *o* in "Tode" is a nicely open Italian *o* (don't forget to do an extra expanding of the breathing muscles on the second note that goes up). The *e* in "Tode" is again mixed with *ö*. The "sein" is a relaxed open *a* with the "in" coming at the very last moment and slightly mixed with *ü*. In the next phrase do exactly the same. On the last phrase, the space in the back of the throat should stay in the same open position throughout the phrase. On the "Tode sein" one should concentrate on using the breath support for a perfect floating *bel canto* line because the notes are quite low for a soprano.

**137**

It goes without saying that these modulations have to be subtle and the original vowel should be pure and still understood. One must at all costs avoid a muffled or darkened sound. If done properly, this will not happen and the voice will sound beautiful, resonant and have a seamless quality from the top to the bottom.

"In the historic international Italianate school *copertura* (covering) describes gradual acoustic adjustments brought about through modifying vowels in the ascending scale ... The larynx is retained in the relatively low position it assumes upon inhalation ... there is no sudden 'shifting of gears' no 'hooking in or over' and no conscious muscular spreading in the pharynx, although there is a sense of openness in the pharynx ... Still, the less conscious effort involved in covering the better" (Richard Miller, Training Tenor Voices).

The expression "covering" (*copertura*) should not be confused with "darkening" (*abdunkeln*). The tone that sounds "darkened", "muffled" or "throaty" is usually caused by the soft palate and uvula being too low, thus obstructing the throat resonance. This is exactly the opposite of the open throat.

Do not open your mouth too wide in the middle register. This is not necessary and will cause the back of the throat to close up. It is possible to sing at least 80% of your vocal range with a half-closed mouth. Try this once: Close your lips to an opening big enough to fit in your index finger. Then sing *a* on an upward scale. The higher you get, the more you will have to open the back of your throat and lift your soft palate. You will be surprised how easy it is to sing the highest notes!

**Good diction**

Consonants are formed by the lips and the front and back parts of the tongue. Vowels are formed exclusively by lifting or flattening the tongue, the only exception being *o* and *u* where the lips are slightly rounded (see exercises).

A singer who is already a complete interpreter and whose foremost priority is to tell the story, will never have problems with diction.

For clear articulation one should make small but strong, precise movements that need not get in the way of your voice production. This must be practised just like everything else – but be sure to keep your throat free and open at all times. Remember that during singing the mouth is not opened further than would be necessary to insert the tip of a finger (except in the very highest notes). This means that the consonants can be articulated quickly and strongly but with the minimum amount of effort. Superfluous movements, such as extravagant gyrations of the lips and opening the mouth too wide because you wrongly assume that this helps your pronunciation, only serve to make the sound woollier and detracts from the beauty of the voice. Clear diction in combination with a free voice production is always possible, once you know how.

## Focus

The singing voice has its space and resonance in the back of the throat, but its placement or focus should always be high and forward. This is called the mask resonance. Most good singers are aware of the importance of the high, forward focus (*der schlanke Sitz*). It should be as evident in a simple song as in the biggest Wagner scene. If you maintain a free and open throat, this should be quite enough to enable the sound to fly freely into the high placement. It is physically impossible to "throw" the sound into the mask resonance by using muscular action. The only way is to "imagine" the sound as a focused laser beam that sits above the ears or between the eyes. This is called the "the illusion of placement". This is where you need a good singing teacher or coach as a monitor who will tell you when the sound is focused correctly. When you get it right you will feel a specific vibration which you should then remember for future use.

**Voice placement**

We maintain that the three most important factors for a healthy voice production are:
* Efficient breath management (*die Atemstütze*) for power and control

**139**

♦ The relaxed and open throat (*der große Rachenraum*) for resonance and beauty
♦ The high placement (*der schlanke Sitz*) for carrying power and focus

**Tip**

One of the most important skills a singer should have is the ability to mark at rehearsals. "Marking" is a well-supported, *piano*, floating tone without any tension in the throat. Some singers can mark in the original range; others prefer to sing an octave down. If you can mark through your role (singing everything piano) this will be the proof that you are using all three – breath support, open throat and focus – optimally. Most singers need to be able to do this sometimes, although it is our experience that great singers often sing full out at all rehearsals.

**Big voices**

Young singers with big voices (the potential Turandots and Siegfrieds), sometimes have difficulty understanding the mask resonance, and will make the tone "narrow" or "small" in their effort to find the focus. Sometimes a potentially dramatic voice will have to start off her professional life by doing Mozart roles. The danger here is that the singer will try to make her natural voice smaller by "narrowing" the voice and thus might get into big trouble. The only thing to do is to maintain the open free throat and concentrate on efficient breath management. If this is done properly, the young singer will find that she can sing wonderfully soft, yet full-bodied floating *piano* notes.

When young singers try this for the first time, they might be disappointed because their voice will sound "thin". The reason for this is that, when you do it properly, the voice is projecting outwards. If you try to make a "big" sound that you can hear beautifully from the inside, it will definitely not reach your audience. Making a recording of your new way of singing might be a pleasant surprise.

The renowned dramatic mezzo Jane Henschel says, "It took a long time for me to discover that a high note, when projected correctly, sounds tiny to me on stage, but is quite loud to the audience" (Dieter David Scholz, Mythos Primadonna).

**Knowledge**

Whereas it may be quite interesting to know the names of the muscles and bones of the vocal apparatus, where they are to be found, and how they function, this knowledge is essentially unimportant. Knowing what the arytenoids or the cricoids do will not bring you one iota nearer to finding the correct way to sing.

## Finding the balance
Singing is an anatomic process and a highly developed skill that requires an acute sense of what is important and what is not. A young singer should learn to find the balance between the many different physical processes that take place during singing. It is not so much a matter of doing something than a matter of knowing exactly what to do. It is a matter of finding the energetic balance, and becoming a finely honed machine able to reach the maximum effect with the minimum of effort.

**Warming up the voice**

Once you have a fairly safe technique and you know which exercises are the best for warming up your voice correctly, you should do your vocal exercises at least five days a week. Before a lesson, a rehearsal or a performance always warm up the voice even if you are only going to sing five notes or speak dialogue. The voice should also be warmed up carefully before attempting difficult vocal exercises. It is important to know exactly how to warm up. When you are doing it right, you do not need hours and hours. It will suffice to do a few effective humming exercises.
The Dictionary of Vocal Terminology defines warming up as "a gradual flexing of the vocal muscles to ease them into movement before subjecting them to

"The length of time necessary to 'warm up' the vocal musculature varies with the technical skill of the individual, the better the technique, the shorter the period of time required to bring the mechanism to a condition of readiness. Those who must warm up for thirty or forty-five minutes do so because of anxiety or compulsion, or in order to impose wrong concepts on a reluctant mechanism" (Cornelius L. Reid, A Dictionary of Vocal Terminology).

higher levels of tension". We would add that the actual vocal muscles or vocal folds (also known as vocal chords) are mostly in perfect working order except for some mucous that accumulates during the night. In our opinion, the muscles that need to be warmed up are in fact the voice-supporting muscles, i.e. the breathing muscles which should be eased into their function exactly as an athlete does before attempting to run the mile. The humming exercises (see below) are especially designed for this purpose. While "warming up", the main concentration should be on the breathing muscles; the vocal folds being quite capable of looking after themselves.

## Exercises

Before you start your exercises in the morning, it is a good idea to limber up the body with stretching exercises; yoga, qigong or the Alexander Technique.

Breathing

Stand straight with your feet as far apart as the shoulders, knees relaxed and head resting comfortably and upright on the shoulders. Breathe in through your mouth and nose, keeping the tongue in a flat, relaxed position and thinking of an *a* vowel to establish the "beginning-of-the-yawn" feeling. Feel how your stomach, flanks, back and chest are slowly filling with air. Hold your breath for five seconds without tensing the throat, tongue, neck or shoulders. Now, while keeping the feeling of expansion, breathe out slowly and imagine that you have a burning candle in front of your mouth, which must be supplied with oxygen, and without the flame going out. Let your breath flow out in a controlled way, keeping the stomach, flank, back and chest muscles expanded as long as possible. With your last breath, push up the inner, lower abdomen muscles and then relax.

Now repeat the exercise by breathing in as quickly as possible in the same way as before and then letting out the breath on "ffffffff" through the relaxed lips again holding the ex-panded stomach, flanks, back and chest as long as possible, without tensing the shoulders, until your breath runs out. Now collapse the breathing muscles and repeat the exercise on the explosive "f-s-f-s-f-s-f" thereby experiencing the *ap-poggio* (the quick "leaning" or expanding of the breathing muscles) on each consonant. Be sure to relax the shoulders, throat and neck as much as possible. Only concentrate on the actual breathing muscles.

The following humming exercises are very valuable. They are used by many singers and singing teachers, although some don't understand the importance of always doing them *piano* and relaxing the throat muscles and the jaw.

**Humming**

Stand as in the previous exercise. Breathe in through mouth and nose while relaxing the tongue and jaw and thinking an *a* vowel. The breathing muscles should expand automatically into their "supporting" position. Close the lips lightly without pressure and imagine a note in the middle register. Now slowly allow the vocal folds to vibrate on the note, thereby producing a soft humming sound. Remember to maintain the open throat and the buoyant, expanded feeling in the body. Do a slow *glissando* on the interval of a fifth, keeping the torso expanded, the throat open and the lips closed.

Repeat the exercise, going down half a note at a time as far as you can without feeling tension in the throat and then go up the scale as high as possible again without feeling any pushing in the throat. If you feel tension in your throat, in-crease the expansion of the breathing musculature or the beginning-of-the-yawn position and try again. It is important to sing as *piano* as possible because only then can one ensure optimal control of the voice. This exercise will help you to feel how the voice is supported by the breath, and how the relaxed open space in the throat helps to free the voice and send it into in the mask.

Now try following exercise. Do it slowly and *piano*. Remember to expand the breathing muscles and keep the open throat even more when you go up.

Now repeat any other simple humming exercises that you might want to try, using the breathing muscles as consciously as possible and keeping the relaxed open throat and relaxed lips. It is important to sing as *piano* and as carefully as possible, listening and observing yourself all the time. Check in the mirror that your shoulders and neck are at all times relaxed.

**Tip**

Do your humming exercises every morning after limbering up. They should be part of your daily routine.

## Finding the natural voice

Start this exercise by doing a few humming scales to get the feeling of the expanded breathing muscles and the free, open throat. Now breathe in and sing an *m* on a relatively high note. Then open the mouth on a relaxed Italian *a* or *o* vowel keeping the breathing muscles expanded. Starting *piano*, slowly swell the tone out in a floating crescendo, and then come back on a decrescendo, ending with the softest tone you can produce without unnecessary tension. Remember to use the breath support to help you keep the voice free and steady throughout the phrase. This is another important daily exercise. If you can perfect the *messa-di-voce* (swelling and diminishing on one tone) you are on your way to being a good singer.

## Finding the mask resonance

Do a few humming exercises to get the correct feeling of the breath supporting the voice and the open throat. Now start an *m* (humming sound) on an easy note in the scale. Once you feel comfortable and the voice is in the right place, open your mouth slightly and sing ma-ma-ma-ma-ma on a descending scale, with a relaxed, open Italian *a* and pausing slightly on the *m*'s.

ma__ ma__ ma__ ma__ ma_____

Do this exercise throughout your vocal range, while "thinking" the tone as high as possible. Exaggerate by putting as much metal as possible into the tone and concentrating on the higher partials while keeping the throat open and supporting with the breath. This should only be done as an exercise to help you feel the vibrations in the mask. When singing on stage you will of course reduce the metal.

Never tense the lips. The relaxed lip position, also called *baciare il suono* (kissing the sound) will help to enhance the beauty and resonance of your voice.

## Practising your vowels

The idea behind this exercise is to sing perfect vowels with the minimum of effort. Some singers are under the false impression that exaggerated lip movements will improve the vowel sounds. This is not so.
It goes without saying that the vowels should be pronounced as in German or Italian.
Stand in front of a mirror and relax your facial muscles, opening the lips just far enough to insert an index finger. Let your jaw drop and relax your tongue. The tip of the tongue lies behind the bottom teeth throughout the exercise.

**145**

Now slowly sing the vowels *a – e – i – o – u* one after the other on one note without breathing in between. Be sure to support the tone with your breath.

The following should happen:
*a*  the tongue is flat
*e*  the middle of the tongue is slightly lifted
*i*  the middle of the tongue is lifted higher
*o*  the tongue flattens slightly and the lips are pursed gently
*u*  the tongue is flat again and the lips are pouted

Practice this as often as possible, striving to sing the purest vowels with the minimum of effort.

**Tip**

When singing in German and French, the *r* is pronounced by vibrating the tip of the tongue against the palate as in Italian. This is different from the spoken language and should be practised. If you have difficulty pronouncing the *r* with the tip of the tongue, try the following exercise: Say *d-t-d-t-d-t-d-t* slowly at first, and then faster and faster until the *r* automatically happens.

## The art of singing

Once you have established a functioning singing technique, it is extremely important not to miss the stage where you must shift focus and start concentrating with all your creative powers on the actual "art" of singing. This is what the profession is all about, and should encompass far more preparation time than learning the anatomical process, which is by far the easiest part. Many young singers miss this point, be-

"The sole purpose of training for the profession of singing is to improve the connection between imagination and the sounds that eventually issue from the singer's mouth" (Thomas Hemsley, Singing and Imagination).

cause they think that they first have to be technically perfect before daring to start on interpretation. This is absolutely wrong, and can set you back precious years. You might even find that you have missed the boat leading to a career, because you have spent too much time on learning "technique" and too little time on learning the actual "art" of singing. It is our experience that most young singers who still have a few technical problems find to their surprise that the problems dissolve as soon as they shift their focus to the interpreting of the music and communicating the magic. "The more common problems of locked knees, locked body and, worst of all, locked breath, can be avoided by focussing, knowledge, involvement and total commitment" (Joan Dornemann, Complete Preparation).

Start working with an experienced coach very early in your artistic development. You have to learn to use your imagination and communicate music and text to your audience as soon as possible.

Tip

**What can a good coach teach you?**
* How to sing recitatives – this needs enormous study
* How to sing rhythmically
* How to sing legato and feel the cadential pulse of the phrase
* How to look for interpretative clues and instructions given by the composer and follow them as accurately as possible. These could be rhythmical changes, *rubati*, *accelerandi*, duration of notes, accents and dynamics
* How to use the words with clear diction and the correct colour and intonation
* The importance of punctuation, i.e. commas or exclamation marks
* The importance of listening to the other singers and harmonies in ensembles
* The importance of listening to the accompaniment, be it piano or orchestra

**147**

# 8 ◆ The Principles of Good Singing

- ◆ How to follow a conductor
- ◆ Being prepared for entrances during arias and ensembles
- ◆ The importance of using your imagination and your creative instincts
- ◆ Matters of taste – musical and dramatic
- ◆ A feeling for the style and period of the specific piece of music
- ◆ Stylistically correct ornamentation for different epochs (baroque, *bel canto*, etc.)
- ◆ Knowledge of possible cuts and differing versions of an opera
- ◆ Performance practice when there is a departure from the written score
- ◆ Freedom and discipline in the right place and perspective

As the singing teacher Arthur Cranner so aptly said: "Never allow a sound to come out of your mouth until it has passed through your mind."

# Acting for the Opera Stage

The singer-actor's task is to combine mental, spiritual, emotional and physical skills in order to portray a complete character on the opera stage, thereby totally engaging the audience from the first to the last row.

The singer-actor must maintain the balance between being completely involved in the story he is telling while still keeping an inner distance to his own emotions. The character (*die Figur*) must be believable and come across naturally without being melodramatic. This is not easy, given the fact that many opera plots might be considered unrealistic and over-the-top, having nothing to do with our daily lives.

**Emotional balance**

But you must remember that the opera stage has its own truth, and when you prepare a role intensively you will find that the emotions on the opera stage are not so far away from real-life emotions.

The singer-actor has to be aware from the very beginning of his training that opera is one of the most complex forms of the performing arts, combining singing, acting, speaking and dancing. These challenges have to be taken into consideration from the first day of your studies.

Already as a student, you must learn to be creative, imaginative and intuitive and at the same time be disciplined and capable of analyzing everything you do.

Before learning an operatic role, it is essential to research the role extensively.
This is done by
* Reading the libretto
* Getting to know the biography of the character
* Doing historical research in the period of the opera
* Analyzing the music

# 9 • Acting for the Opera Stage

## The libretto

Read through the whole piece. This not only helps to get a feeling for the surroundings of your character but it can also give valuable clues if your character is referred when you are not actively on stage. In some cases it is even necessary to read through other operas, for instance in the case of Loge in *Das Rheingold*. Not only is he referred to in his own musical "Leitmotiv" throughout the opera, but he is also referred to in *Die Walküre*, when Wotan calls him to create the fire that surrounds Brünnhilde. If you are singing the Contessa in *Le nozze di Figaro* it will also be valuable to read through the libretto of Rossini's *Il Barbiere di Siviglia*, because you will get an insight into the beginnings of the love affair between Rosina and Conte Almaviva. To this end you should, of course, know that the Contessa in *Le nozze di Figaro* is the Rosina in *Il Barbiere di Siviglia*.

We have to repeat what we have already said in earlier chapters. It is most important that you learn to speak fluently the opera languages in which you have to sing. This is one of the essential skills of a professional singer.

After having read through the opera, try to tell the story out loud in your own words. In this way, you will soon find out whether you have really understood the story. It is also important to inquire into the meanings of the terminology you haven't heard of before.

A good example of this is in Max's aria from *Der Freischütz*. He talks about his love for the forest and of hunting a *"Sechzehnender"*. You cannot portray the character of the hunter, Max, without knowing exactly what a *Sechzehnender* (a sixteen-point buck) looks like, and without being able to feel the pride of a man who is lucky enough to hunt down and shoot such a rare animal. You might find examples in world literature and the fine arts. Your private dislike of hunting should not play a role in your interpretation.

## The biography of the character

The following "W"-questions might help you to analyze the character of a role and its function in the opera. It is important to assess the situation scene by scene and act by act. Don't count the events or emotions that are still to happen. Look at the single situation of the present moment. The character does not know the future either!

As an example, we will analyze Valentin's aria from the 1st act of Gounod's *Faust*:

* Who am I?
  - A brave soldier
  - Devout, with strong moral values
  - Patriotic and duty-bound
  - The elder brother of Marguerite
  - An orphan (our mother is dead)
* Where have I come from?
  - From town
  - From the house where I live together with my sister
* Where am I, who is with me, what are my feelings?
  - I am standing in front of the inn at the town gate
  - My best friend – a young student called Siebel – is with me. He will look after my sister when I have to go to war
  - We meet Wagner and other students
  - Another man (Mephisto) joins us
  - I don't know him but distrust him instinctively
  - When we all drink together he conjures up wine and drinks a toast to Marguerite
  - I don't like the way he talks
  - I don't like his magic tricks
  - I fight him
  - My sword is powerless against him
  - I banish him by putting the sign of the cross on him
  - I recognize the devil in him

◆ What is important to me?
- I have to protect my sister's virginity
- I have to protect my own honour
- I want to become a brave soldier, fearless and with trust in God
◆ Where am I going?
- I go to war

You will, of course, be aware of the fact that Valentin dies at the end of the opera, while cursing his sister for being with child. But, as we mentioned above, this should not play a role in the interpretation of the first aria, because Valentin is not aware of his future. The same applies to characters like Butterfly or Posa (*Don Carlos*). Beware of falling into the trap of anticipating the later destinies or emotions of your character. This will muddle the biographical line and above all confuse your audience!

**The text as a play** After reading through the libretto once, it is a very good idea to read through the words of your part without the music. Try to read it like an actress would read a play. This is much more difficult than you think because you will have the musical rhythms in your mind. Nonetheless, it is very important that you ignore the music for once and speak the part as an actor would, with exclamation marks, question marks, natural pauses and especially with speaking rhythms which might differ from the singing rhythms. This helps tremendously to get a natural feeling for the interpretation of the text. If the text is very old-fashioned, it might help to translate it into everyday language or into your own language (if it is in a language foreign to you). Then write it down and speak the text as if you have to act the part on the spoken stage.

## The history

Read as much as you can about the opera. This could be the original book upon which the libretto is based, but it can also be novels based in the same historic period. If you are doing one of the roles in *Le nozze di Figaro* or *Il Barbiere di Siviglia*, you would naturally read the original plays by Beaumarchais. Thus you will get a feeling for the history and the surroundings in which the opera is taking place.

Look at pictures of costumes and go to art galleries. Specifically look at the gestures and postures of the time in which the opera is based. Find out about the historical periods in Europe, for instance the *Biedermeier* period in which many German operas like *Der Wildschütz* or *Der Waffenschmied* are set. Further examples are the operas of Richard Strauss, where it is most important to understand what Vienna was like when the class system was still prevalent, as in for example *Der Rosenkavalier* or *Arabella*. If you are preparing a role in one of these operas you should definitely read the letters exchanged between Strauss and his librettist Hugo von Hofmannsthal for many valuable clues about the characters and the times in which they lived.

## The musical clues

Look at the directions given by the composer. For instance why does Verdi write the little pauses in "caro nome che'il – mio – cor" which Gilda sings after meeting Gualtier Maldé for the first time? Obviously, she is absolutely breathless with adolescent love. This should be understood and conveyed when singing the aria. In the aria where Susanna helps Cherubino dress in women's clothes, there are funny little skipping motifs in the orchestration which might indicate that Cherubino is trying to walk in the dress and probably trips on these notes. Listen to the orchestra and analyze why certain instruments have been chosen by the composer. What do they have to do with your character? Search for musical clues like tempo changes, rhythm changes, accents and so on. Once you have done your research you can start learning the part musically with your coach, because you will now automatically take all these interpretative clues into consideration and be able to create a role completely with all its many facets. An experienced coach will be essential for this work!

"It is my experience that singers who start by vocalizing, and then try to add the words later, rarely achieve the clear, imaginative declamation of the text that all vocal music requires. The accurate and subtle matching of vocal tone to the sentiments to be expressed will probably never be fully realized" (Thomas Hemsley, Singing and Imagination).

After having explored the historical background and becoming acquainted with the person that you have to portray, both dramatically and musically, you will now be so secure that you will also be able to reject these ideas if necessary and react flexibly to the demands of a stage director (*der Regisseur*) who might even go as far as deciding to stage the exact opposite of the conventional interpretation. The beginner should never underestimate the importance of a solid background of knowledge as a basis to start with!

## Creating a role on stage

The requirements for creating a role on stage are your inner experience plus the acting handcraft.

Acting classes

You will have to practice these inner skills as well as the acting handcraft step by step in acting classes. They cannot be learned from a book. We can only draw your attention to it. We therefore strongly recommend that you take part in acting workshops or work individually with teachers who are not only well versed in the basics of acting and stagecraft but are also aware of the specific needs of an actor who also has to sing.

A complete knowledge of your own inner experiences plus the practical acting handcraft is an essential prerequisite for becoming an efficient singer-actor.

Your acting teacher should be just as important to you as your singing teacher and can be of great help to you throughout your singing career.

The inner experience means
* The inner emotional dialogue (you can also call it the inner contact) with your colleagues and the audience
* The understanding of the stage as a space for interaction
* The focussing of your energy to project the message of the role clearly and directly

## The fundamental dramatic truth

Without an initial thought there can be no valid gesture, facial expression, movement or word on stage! Without a good motive, there is no convincing action! This is the fundamental dramatic truth.

When Cherubino jumps onto an unsteady chair to catch the ribbon of his beloved Contessa out of Susanna's hand in the 1st act of *Le nozze di Figaro* his thought before he jumps might be: "I desperately want to catch the ribbon. I want to have at least one thing which reminds me of my Contessa, whom I love so much." With this thought in mind, which happens in less than a second, the Cherubino singer-actor will have the right verve to transmit his truth and message of the action. A thought such as "I feel uncomfortable with an unsteady chair" would change the meaning of his action completely and distract the audience's attention.

The initial thought before a gesture or movement of feet, hands, head or eyes, before using a prop or touching a person is the basic acting "credo" on stage. Everything else is a lie. To prepare these initial thoughts you must read the libretto and analyze the character and the music, as already described.

# 9 • Acting for the Opera Stage

## Subtext

**An important tool** The subtext is one of the most important tools of a singer-actor. It is the thoughts and feelings that underlie the actual sung text. When the Contessa sings her big aria *Dove sono, i bei momenti, di dolcezza e di piace,* she is literally saying, "Where are they, these moments of sweetness and pleasure?" What she is thinking is far more complex. She is remembering how romantic the days of young love were. She can smell and feel Almaviva and she remembers all the wonderful words he used to whisper in her ear during their courtship. Many thoughts and feelings go through her mind as she sings these few words.

> Never walk onto the stage for an audition, a rehearsal or a performance without having prepared the role or aria with subtexts (inner thoughts)!

Obviously she will have used these thoughts to create the character during the rehearsals. Once it comes to the performance, she can put the thoughts into the drawer called "subconscious" and will be free to let the music soar. A singer-actor who uses the subtext with imagination will be far more interesting to listen to than the one who is simply singing the given words. A young singer learning a part for the first time should analyze every single phrase he sings and write out the subtext before attempting to interpret the music. Thus the voice will have far more colour and nuance and the character will come to life.

## Listening

In most opera roles, every singer, even those singing main roles, will find that he or she probably stands and listens more than he actually sings on stage. One of the most important skills that every singer should learn is to listen with the same focus that he uses when singing.

If you are really inside your character and you stay within the story that is being told, you will never be able just to stand around doing nothing. Being your private self on stage is taboo! You can be sure that an audience knows exactly when you are being sincere in the role and when you are just being yourself. Besides, it is very unprofessional and distracting to your colleagues!

An example for acting through listening is the role of Marcellina in the 1st act of *Le nozze di Figaro* during Dr. Bartolo's aria. She does not have a single note to sing but has to listen and to watch carefully what Bartolo says. Marcellina wants to marry Figaro and Dr. Bartolo could be the only one to help her achieve this goal. Maybe she loves her old master

> Listening means being actively involved in the story!

(read the libretto of *Il Barbiere di Siviglia*!), maybe she trusts him, maybe she distrusts him, maybe she thinks he is showing off – in any case she starts listening to him as soon as he starts his aria. And she listens by using subtext! Her subtext will show her feelings and thoughts about Bartolo silently, for example: "I need him; nobody else is here to help me. Maybe he will be successful. He wants to have his revenge on Figaro. No, he is getting old. Actually he has no ideas. He only pretends to be clever! But I have no choice! I must not show him my doubts! I must pretend to believe him. Otherwise I will lose my last support. I decide to believe in his strength!" This is only one example for this scene. She could choose many other thoughts, depending on the stage director's concept.

## Observing people

Before working on your stage skills, you should start observing people in everyday situations. Before a sculptor starts forming a figure out of clay, he first has to look carefully at the object he wants to create or recreate. In your profession you will be expected to portray a variety of characters. They will be young, old, disabled, pretty, ugly, happy, sad, energetic, passive or hysterical. A woman might also have to play the part of a man or vice-versa.

Study human beings in their everyday life. What is the difference between the body language of a man and a woman? How does an old man walk? Look at the details. Every lift of an elbow, every facial expression, every gesture or stance is important. Can one guess the emotions of somebody from the way they walk? A quick walk may tell you that a person is nervous or purposeful, and a low, languid walk might express sensuality or just laziness. Try to notice the subtle differences. What do people do with their eyes? When they lie or are nervous, they might make rapid eye movements or when they feel happy the corners of their eyes and mouth might crinkle.

A mezzo who is studying a trouser part or pant's role (*die Hosenrolle*) should analyze the way a young, confident man walks. How big are his steps, are the knees relaxed or stiff, does he use his arms and hands differently than a young woman would?

Then go home and try everything out in front of a mirror. Practise expressing your emotions through body language. Practise using your facial muscles to show a variety of emotions.

Above all, practise expressing emotions with your eyes.

Never forget to keep a critical distance from yourself. Try to look at what you are doing from the outside and listen to the comments of trusted friends and colleagues concerning your stage behaviour and appearance.

## The eyes

The eyes are probably the most useful tool that a singer-actor has at his disposal.

"The eyes, more than any other part of the body, reveal the mental process: if they wander, we feel the mind is wandering; if they search, we feel the mind is searching; and if they focus strongly, we feel the mind is focused strongly" (Wesley Balk, The Complete Singer-Actor).

# Eye Focus

What you think will be projected through your eyes. Your eyes are the most powerful guide for the audience to understand your thinking and feeling processes.

There are two main categories of eye focus that can be used by the singer-actor:

* The direct or extroverted focus
* The inward or introverted focus

The direct focus is used when one is addressing someone or looking at something of interest. In a narrative aria like "O, zittre nicht, mein lieber Sohn" the Königin der Nacht (Queen of the Night) is speaking directly to Tamino, and when Ännchen tells the story "Einst träumte meiner sel'gen Base" she uses the direct focus because she is telling Agathe a story. An object of interest could be a letter like in Charlotte's big aria from *Werther*. This focus is fairly easy. The singer-actor need only direct his thoughts towards the listener or the object.

**Direct focus**

The inward focus would be used for instance in the aria "Ach ich fühl's" from *Die Zauberflöte*, where Pamina is alone with her thoughts and memories. Another instance would be the Contessa arias from *Le nozze di Figaro*. This introverted eye focus is more difficult than the extroverted focus. We have all seen it in everyday life. Your mother is standing in the kitchen and her movements are suddenly arrested because she is thinking of something. It could be tomorrow's shopping list or the argument she has had with your father that morning. She is totally concentrated within herself and the eye focus has turned inward. There is a stillness and total concentration on the inner thought processes. The eyes are open but are not directed at anything.

**Inward focus**

When you are interpreting a role or aria, it goes without saying that there will always be shifting modes of focus, for instance Butterfly might start off telling Suzuki that Pinkerton will come back one fine day, but at a certain point the aria will become an inner monologue. The Königin der Nacht (Queen

**Shifting modes of focus**

of the Night) will start her aria by directing her eye focus at Tamino, but when she starts talking about her own unhappiness and distress, her eye focus will turn inward. The secret is to be very exact about when and how the different eye focuses are implemented.

To start off with, a young singer-actor should prepare this analytically. When he is more experienced, the momentary inspiration will be enough for him to know exactly how to use the eye focus. At the beginning he should read the text carefully and look for the transition points where the emotions or the music change. These points must be written down and carefully practised.

The direct focus serves to give the audience a point of interest outside of the singer-actor and the inward focus, if done correctly, will pull the audience's attention towards you. We are always surprised at our workshops, how much more powerful the inward eye focus is compared to the normal direct eye focus. Especially during auditioning, this focus can be very valuable. Not only will you engage your audience but, by staying within your own or the character's thoughts, you will be much less nervous.

**Tip**

No eye focus, whether direct or inward, can be effective without the thought that comes first!

The following is not acceptable:
◆ Closed eyes
Never close your eyes on stage unless you want to send a specific message. From the beginning you should guard against this bad habit. Especially during the inward focus, the eyes should nevertheless always be seen by the audience.
◆ Staring eyes
Wide-open and staring eyes are also taboo. Unless you want to show extreme fear or astonishment, you should be careful of opening your eyes unnaturally wide. Some singers tend to do this when they sing a high note!

◆ Wandering eyes

Eyes that continually shift focus can be very distracting to an audience because it sends the message that you are not concentrated. It is interesting to note that when nine people are standing on stage listening intently to the person singing an aria the tenth person who is not listening and who is just looking aimlessly around will be immediately noticed by the audience.

A good example for using the eye focus and the subtext is Ellen Orford's embroidery aria from the 3rd act of *Peter Grimes* by Benjamin Britten. We include the scenes with Captain Balstrode before and after the aria. This is only one of the many valid possibilities for interpreting this scene (see p. 162f.).

## The facial gesture

What you do with your face is just as important as the eye focus. The facial expression (*die Mimik*) is a universal language that can be understood by all peoples and cultures. When a baby in Turkey smiles he will lift up the corners of his mouth exactly as a baby in Mexico does.

Peter Matic and
Richard Salter
in *Das Schloss* by
Aribert Reimann

# 9 • Acting for the Opera Stage

| Sung text | Focus | Subtext (of the person who sings) |
|---|---|---|
| *Ellen:*<br>"Is the boat in?" | Directed at Balstrode | I am worried about Grimes. |
| *Balstrode:*<br>"Yes – for more than an hour. Peter seems to have disappeared. Not in his boat, not in his hut." | Directed at Ellen | I don't know what happened, I fear the worst – Grimes' death. |
| *Ellen:*<br>"This I found down by the tidemark" | Directed at Balstrode (showing him the boy's jersey) | I am worried about the boy. |
| *Balstrode:*<br>"The boy's!" | Directed at Ellen | The boy must be dead. |
| *Ellen:*<br>"My broidered anchor on the chest" | Looks at the jersey (sweater) then at Balstrode; then her focus turns inward shortly before the aria starts. | It is his jersey. I fear for his life. |
| *Aria:*<br>"Embroidery in childhood was a luxury of idleness. A coil of silken thread giving dreams of a silk, of a silk and satin life. Now my broidery affords the clue who's meaning we avoid! | Inward focus | I see myself as a child. I wanted a better life. I had so many dreams.<br><br>This will have an awful end. |
| My hand remembered its old skill. These stitches tell a curious tale. | | I haven't done embroidery for a long time but I remember everything. |
| I remember I was brooding on the fantasies of children, and dreamt that only by wishing I could bring some silk into their lives. Now my broidery affords the clue now my broidery affords ... Now my broidery affords the clue who's meaning we avoid!" | A short look to Balstrode; then her focus turns inward until the end of the aria. | I hoped to bring joy into the lives of children, but I was too naïve.<br><br>Something awful must have happened. ... I don't want to admit it. The boy must be dead. |

| Sung text | Focus | Subtext (of the person who sings) |
|---|---|---|
| *Balstrode*: <br> "We'll find him, <br> maybe give him a hand." | Directed at Ellen | I want to comfort her and give her hope. |
| *Ellen*: <br> "We have no power to help him now <br> we have no power …" | Directed at Balstrode | I have no strength left. |
| *Balstrode*: <br> "We have the power, <br> we have the power. <br> In the black moment, when your <br> friend suffers unearthly torment, <br> we cannot turn our backs <br> when horror breaks one heart <br> all hearts are broken, all are broken." | Directed at Ellen <br><br> To himself <br> Inward focus | I want to hope. <br> But – <br> I am losing my faith. <br> The boy is dead and <br> Grimes? <br> I must pull myself together. <br> But I despair. |
| *Together*: <br> "We shall be there with him, <br> we shall be there with him, <br> we shall be with him." | Ellen looks towards the coast. <br> Balstrode turns his focus inward. | E.: I have to help Peter. <br> B.: I will be lonely. |
| *Balstrode*: <br> "Nothing to do but wait, <br> since the solution is beyond life, <br> beyond dissolution. | To himself | I am helpless. |

As a result of the correct eye focus, the facial gesture should happen nearly automatically. Don't pull faces! As long as the thoughts and emotions behind your actions on stage are honest, you will convince your audience to the last row. "The face is capable of reflecting an enormous palette of emotions … Many singers are afraid of using even a fraction of the power in their faces as they sing. Some believe that using their faces in singing distorts their vocalism … It is only through regular exercise of facial expressive capacities while singing that singers will be able to discover

> The facial gesture is an essential part of the eye focus and both should be practised consistently in front of a mirror.

**163**

how to use those capacities and not destroy their vocal capabilities through unwanted tension" (Helfgot/Beeman, The Third Line).

## Gestures

What should I do with my hands?! This is a big problem for a beginner who is standing on stage for the first time. Usually he falls into the trap of the "hands-on-hips" gesture which is *verboten*. Even when you are singing Carmen!

Here are a few rules to help you overcome this difficulty:

* Less is more. Doing nothing, is often much stronger than doing too much
* Don't use half-hearted gestures. If you start a gesture, take it through to the end
* Rather no gesture, than the wrong one
* One strong gesture is more effective than three small gestures
* Don't repeat gestures which were effective once. This will only weaken your message
* A gesture should not be too long or too short – just long or short enough to be effective
* Observe people on the streets and try to understand the emotions behind their stance or gestures. Then copy these natural gestures
* Observe experienced colleagues and ask them to help you
* Practise in front of a mirror

At the beginning, you can solve the problem by using a prop. A fan, a walking stick or handbag can be used very effectively to cover your inexperience. Ask the stage director or his assistant for help.

The most important rule of all – never use a gesture without the thought or feeling that comes before. A gesture which is not supported by a thought can only be an empty gesture and will mean nothing to the audience.

# Posture

Posture is influenced by:
* The character you are portraying
* Your breath support
* The stage itself
* Your shoes

### The character

The role is, of course, the most important factor to influence your posture. If you are singing Rigoletto you will walk like a hunchback, and if you are singing the Duke you will walk with a royal bearing. It is important to find a stance which you will be able to keep up for the whole evening.

### Breath support

As a singer, it is particularly important to find a posture that does not hinder your breath support. Even if you have to lie on a sofa or sit on the floor, you must see to it that your torso is held in a position that enables your voice to function smoothly.

Helga Dernesch and Isoldé Elchlepp in *Bernarda Albas Haus* by Aribert Reimann

Supporting the breath efficiently is possible during most actions on stage – the only exception being when you are bent forward. In this case, you should see to it that you straighten out before singing.

* Don't make yourself smaller than you are. If you happen to be six feet tall, even if you are a woman, then be proud of it! Nothing is worse than trying to hide this fact by pulling in your head, rounding your shoulders or bending your knees.
* If you are standing in profile, see that your body is open to the audience. Your front leg (downstage leg) should be slightly more to the back than the back leg (upstage leg). If

Tips

you are kneeling, you should kneel on the downstage leg, so that your body is open to the public.

* Female singers should be aware that in most operas it is unacceptable to cross your legs when sitting down.

* Beware of keeping rhythm with your body. Nothing is worse than seeing a singer tapping his foot or moving his hands or body in time with the music. Learn to count in your head without showing it to the audience.

* When you walk on the stage it is sometimes useful to lean back slightly (*die Rückverlagerung*). This is especially helpful if you are wearing a long dress.

* Shoes are one of the most important factors that influence your stance. During rehearsals, always wear your original or similar shoes. You will never get the feeling for a part if you wear thick-soled sneakers (unless called for in the role).

Women will very often be expected to wear high heels. Most young girls today are not used to this, and it is important for them to practise walking naturally on high heels.

♦ Wear rehearsal clothes that are similar to your costume. A Cherubino should rehearse in trousers, a Susanna in a dress of the appropriate length. Not only does this give you a feeling for the part, but also helps your colleagues. They will get used to treating you differently, and they might also have to grab your skirt or tussle with you as part of the stage action.

♦ From the beginning of your studies you should train your body to do everything that might be expected of you on stage. You will have to climb up ladders, do acrobatic tricks, hang on a trapeze ten meters high while singing a difficult aria or walk down a sharply slanted stage. We have seen all of this on opera stages in Germany. Keep your body fit and well-trained. Practise your balance by using a trampoline. When you walk downstairs, practise doing this without looking down. You will have to do this often and it is extremely difficult.

## Portraying emotions

It is very difficult for a young singer to find a way of showing the feeling of the character on stage without being overwhelmed by their emotions.

There are many schools of thought on how to learn the process of transporting your emotions to an audience. The "method" acting of Lee Strasberg, which was made famous by Marlon Brando, expects from the actor to remember an incident where he felt the same emotions that his character is experiencing, and then reproduce them while portraying the character. This is not recommended for singers. It is far easier to start from the outside. If you have difficulty reproducing the feelings of your character, you might want to

Kate Reid says "Acting is not being emotional but being able to express emotion".

"An emotional performer is often the product of an expressive face" (Mark Ross Clark in: Singing, Acting and Movement in Opera).

**167**

Creating emotions

start by first trying out the facial expression of the particular moment. For instance, if you are supposed to be extremely sad, try looking into the mirror and making exaggerated facial gestures conveying sadness. You will often find that this will produce the emotion.

Another way of conveying particular emotions could be to think of an unrelated situation with similar emotions.

We knew a soprano who had to sing Violetta once with a tenor who was particularly obnoxious and unattractive. Asked afterwards how she managed to show her love so convincingly, she said: "All I thought about was how wonderful it is to eat a piece of delicious chocolate cake!" The fact is that her "feeling" while imagining the chocolate cake was absolutely true and sincere. That is why it worked.

It can be very dangerous to allow yourself to be overwhelmed by the emotions of your character.

**A case in point**

Losing emotional control during a performance is considered to be unprofessional.

We once saw a performance of *Madam Butterfly* where the singer was doing the title role for the first time. She did not have her emotions under control and started sobbing bitterly in the aria where she has to send her child away. Of course her vocal line went to pieces! What she really should have done was to let out the emotion in the earlier rehearsals (even if she found it embarrassing in front of her colleagues) and then learnt to control it with technique.

## Laughing and crying

When you have to laugh onstage it should be as natural as possible. For instance, when Norina in *Don Pasquale* reads about the melodramatic cavalier in her book and has to burst out laughing, this should be a real laugh coming from your belly and not an artificial melodious laugh. It will help to listen to a recording of yourself.

Crying on stage is one of the most difficult things that a young singer has to do. It is a good idea to learn how to do it mechanically first. Laughing and crying are based on the same physical process. Take a deep breath and start panting like a dog, using your diaphragm to push out the air in quick, strong urges. Then close your vocal folds adding the sound and you will find that it sounds like laughing or crying. Now you can start varying the different laughing and crying sounds by adding different emotions.

**The same physical process**

Some young singers might find it extremely difficult to be in close bodily contact with their stage partners. On the opera stage you may have to wear seductive see-through clothes and revealing costumes. You might be expected to embrace and even passionately kiss your partner. Men might have to fight each other in close combat or might be expected to perform lewd acts with their female partners. In some roles you will have to be extremely seductive, and in others you might have to whip somebody on stage. This will often be at odds with your private nature.

**Physical contact on stage**

Nonetheless, it is extremely important that you learn to do these things with great courage and conviction. Embracing or kissing someone should be learnt technically during the acting class. Looking somebody in the eye for a long time is also one of the things that first have to be practised coolly and technically.

It will help you to consider clearly and with concentration, that it is the character who is doing these acts and not your private self. Besides, practising highly emotional scenes over and over again will make them easier to do. It is not a good idea to avoid doing them honestly at rehearsals. The stage director and colleagues will only lose their patience with you.

# 9 ✦ Acting for the Opera Stage

**Concentration and focus**

One of the most important things that a young singer-actor must learn is to focus on the task at hand. During a performance, your priority should always be on portraying the character and conveying the emotional message of the music, and nothing else. The other things like doing the moves, looking at the conductor or handling props should be on autopilot. That is what rehearsals are for: to learn this kind of discipline and focus. Do not allow yourself to be distracted by unimportant things happening around you. We often meet young singers who are always going on about how bad their colleagues are and how much the conductor irritates them. This only serves to distract them from learning the inner focus that is so essential for being a singing performer onstage. During the rehearsals they should concentrate rather on learning to use the props, finding out what the conductor wants and trying out different vocal ideas so that when it comes to the performance, these actions become part of the subconscious mind.

**Tip**

If you want to be treated with respect by your singing colleagues and by the musical and scenic staff, then you should also treat them with respect. Try to get involved in the ideas of the conductor or stage director without prejudice.

**Thought-lines**

At any given moment during a performance, the singer-actor's mind is constantly filled with many different thoughts and emotions. They can be "I am feeling so sad because he has left me" or "Damn, my moustache is coming off" or "The high note is coming up, so I have to give more breath support" or "It feels so wonderful to be in love with Alfredo" or "On the next bar comes the strong chord where I have to get up from the floor so I have to tense my muscles on the bar before, so as not to be too late with this action" or "I have to pick up the glass exactly three bars from now, so I must start walking over to the table now" or "How wonderful it feels to be singing this glorious phrase. I am honouring Verdi by putting my whole soul into his music" or "This is where I have to start counting five bars to enable me to sing the next cue on time" or "I am really enjoying doing this dance with all my heart and soul". We call these the "thought-lines".

Although the main part of one's energies will always be concentrated on portraying the music and the character, these thoughts will be underlying and can be stronger or weaker depending on how one organizes them. The singer-actor has to learn to keep the thought-lines in little drawers in his subconscious mind and decide which drawer should be opened when it is needed. For example when the Contessa is singing the recitative to her big aria, *Dove sono*, she will concentrate on colouring each word or sentence with the appropriate sentiments and feelings and might at the same time have to think of certain actions that she has to perform. As soon as she starts singing the actual aria, her concentration and priority will be on the glorious music and the beautiful vocal line. The emotions will be conveyed to the audience through Mozart's music while the innate musicality of the singer will enable her to give the correct colouring and accents. This will be enough to make the magic come across. A young singer-actor has to learn to set priorities and should know which thought-line is important at every given moment.

## Spoken dialogue

It goes without saying that you have to speak the language perfectly before you can speak dialogue on stage. After having mastered the language, you could perfect your dialogue by doing the following:

# 9 ◆ Acting for the Opera Stage

◆ Read through your part as well as that of your scene partner. Analyze the emotional content of the text and write out the subtext.

◆ Take the text seriously. This can sometimes be very difficult if the words are banal as in some operettas or very old-fashioned as is frequently the case in opera. Always be aware of the fact that the stage character takes his words seriously.

◆ While learning the text take into consideration every comma, period, exclamation or question mark. These punctuation marks will influence the melody of your sentence. For instance, the voice would go up at the end of a question and might get louder when the sentence ends in an exclamation mark.

◆ Tempo and timing! Do not allow a gap if you are reacting to a protagonist. Once you have taken up the flow of the dialogue, you may use tempo changes to portray certain emotions within your own lines but be careful not to leave long boring gaps. Learn to think ahead. This rule also counts for singing recitatives.

◆ Do not speak too softly on stage. The same resonance, power and breath support that you use for singing should also be used when speaking dialogue. It is also a good idea to speak more slowly and clearly than in normal offstage speech. Even if you know your text, the audience doesn't!

◆ Warm up your voice before speaking on stage.

## Tradition

A case in point

We once attended a rehearsal of *Hänsel und Gretel,* where the Gretel was an American soprano who was singing the part for the first time. She spoke excellent German and sang the role very well. At the rehearsal she started complaining about the German text, which to her ears sounded extremely old-fashioned. She suggested changing the text to make it more modern. The *Regisseur* had to explain to her that practically every German child grows up with the original fairy tale and

172

at least every second German child grows up listening to Humperdinck's opera. They all know the text by heart because it is a part of their cultural tradition. It would have been sacrilege to change even one word! I don't think we have to comment on this little anecdote.

## Props

The more unusual your props, the more you will have to practise with them.

• Practise carrying your props. Very often a suitcase or a basket is supposed to be heavy but the props master has in actual fact not made it heavy enough. Then you should at least convey the idea of weight to the audience.

• Treat your props naturally. If the Knusperhexe (witch) in *Hänsel und Gretel* has to open the oven door, she has to show that her hands are burning even if the door is not really hot. If you have to hold your rapier or sword in both hands do this very carefully because the audience should think that the sword is sharp.

• Practise opening and closing clasps and locks. It can be very embarrassing for a Figaro to fumble at his barber's case when he needs to shave Bartolo on cue.

• When reading, do not move your head from side to side or move your lips. Only amateurs do this. If you have observed people reading a book or a letter you will have noticed that they only move their eyes.

• Practise using costume props like capes or gloves. When Violetta is singing her big aria and the director tells her to put on her gloves at the same time this has to be practised time and again at rehearsals because it could spoil the whole tragedy of the aria if she starts fumbling. Even helping somebody into a coat can turn out to be a disaster if you do not prepare the coat so that you are not holding it upside down or the person getting into the coat misses the sleeves because you are not holding it properly.

◆ Arms and weapons. At least once in your career you will have to use a knife, a sword or a dagger, especially if you are male. But even female singer-actors will have to use weapons, for example, Oktavian, who has to fight with Baron Ochs or Tosca who has to kill Scarpia. We recommend that you take classes in fencing and other theatre fighting techniques if your music school does not offer it.

**Tip**

If you want to put a sword into its scabbard without looking down, it is a good idea to hold the top of the scabbard with your one hand and with the other hand guide the sword down, at the same time catching the point of the sword with the fingers of the hand holding the scabbard. Thus you prevent embarrassing attempts at finding the opening of the scabbard.

**Fans**

Using a fan (*der Fächer*) naturally on stage is extremely difficult and takes a lot of practise. While still students, female singers should buy themselves a costume fan and find somebody to show them how to use fan language. One cannot start practising too early! You will be singing many roles where a fan is going to be an essential prop. You can send thousands of different messages if you have learnt the fan language. You can show anger by tapping the closed fan in the palm of your hand or you can seduce somebody by opening the fan slowly and then covering the bottom half of your face while flirting with your eyes.

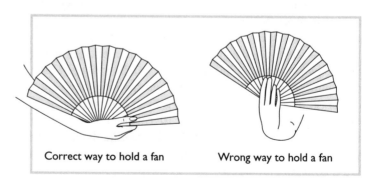

Correct way to hold a fan        Wrong way to hold a fan

In roles where you have to use a fan often, the fan should become the extension of your arm. It should hang on a loop which has exactly the correct length to enable you to catch the fan and bring it up to your face in one graceful movement. The cardinal rule is to use the fan only when necessary, and avoid hectic, unmotivated and unnatural fanning. This can be very distracting and is one of the deadly theatre sins.

Tie a knot in the fan ribbon so that when the fan hangs loosely from your wrist, the top part of the fan is exactly in the centre of the palm of your hand. Now, with your arm hanging down and the back of your hand turned to the front, take hold of the frame attached to the first fold with your thumb and second finger and at the same time bring up your arm and shake your wrist gently to allow the fan to unfold. Catch the last fold with your small finger so that the fan stays open. Now turn your wrist and bring the fan up in front of you with the thumb on the outside and the other fingers turned in towards you. To close the fan, let your wrist fall forward and the fan will automatically fall close. You can also use your other hand to close the fan, depending on the dramatic situation. Practise these actions so that they become part of you. Practise doing them fast and slow and experiment using the fan to accentuate certain dramatic actions.

**The fan technique**

## The spotlight

Professional singers always know exactly where the spot light is and how to manoeuvre themselves into the light so that they can be seen clearly by the audience. Sometimes you need only go back or forward one step to be in the light.

## Dancing on stage

This is an essential skill for every singer-actor. In practically every second opera you will have to waltz (e.g. *Arabella, La*

*Traviata* and all operettas) or perform a historical dance like the fandango in *Le nozze di Figaro* or an Elizabethan dance in Britten's *Gloriana*. You might also have to do dance routines in the many musicals that are performed in smaller houses in Germany. You should take lessons with an expert.

## Being considerate

Always be aware of your partner

♦ When you have to cross the stage and the partner is singing, then cross behind him or, if you have to cross in front, do it quickly when he is not singing.

♦ Don't upstage your stage partners! This is another one of the deadly theatre sins. Upstaging means when you place yourself in a position which is unfavourable for your partner. Such as when he has to sing an important aria and you, as the listener place yourself upstage from him, forcing him to sing with his back to the audience!

♦ Don't distract from an important aria or situation in which you are not directly involved by unnecessary movements or actions which have nothing to do with the scene.

♦ When you have to grab hold of your stage partner or have to fight him, you should always be aware that you have to do this in a controlled way that looks brutal to the audience, but is an actual fact a rehearsed action. You don't want wigs

to get mussed or false noses to fly off because you have forgotten what has been so carefully rehearsed. A famous example is the slap that Conte Almaviva gives Figaro in the fourth act of *Le nozze di Figaro*. In actual fact he wants to slap Cherubino but the latter ducks in time and the Conte slaps Figaro by accident. Not only does the timing of Cherubino and Figaro have to be perfect, but the slap can only work if the Conte pulls his arm back strongly, creating an impression of power and then just touches Figaro lightly. The onus is always on the one who is being slapped. Figaro has to react strongly by throwing his head back as if he has really been slapped and at the same time he has to generate the slapping sound by clapping his hands together without the audience noticing.

We once heard a story about a *Tosca* performance where it was fairly obvious to the audience that during the second act Scarpia and Tosca hated each other privately.

A case in point

During her famous aria Scarpia was silently served a tray of things to eat and drink, whereupon he proceeded to clatter and clink the cutlery and crockery, thus distracting the audience completely from her aria. Needless to say the Tosca was furious. The legend goes that she bribed the props master at the next performance and when Scarpia started eating, he discovered to his aggravation, that every single plate, knife, fork and glass had been firmly glued to the tray!

## Bowing or curtsying

The way you bow or curtsy depends on costume, period and character. A chambermaid wearing a short dress would do a quick bob (*der Knicks*), and a countess wearing a long full skirt would do a deep curtsy (*die Verbeugung* or *die Reverenz*). In both cases, the left leg takes the weight of the body and the right leg is swept behind the left. Then the knees are bent either quickly for the bob or slowly and deeply for the curtsy. In both cases, it is essential that you keep a straight back. Nothing is worse than seeing somebody curtsy with their behind sticking out! When you are doing a deep curtsy and have to stay in this position for some time, it is permissible to rest your right leg on your left calf under the voluminous skirt.

The gentleman in period costume would put his right leg forward with a straight knee and a pointed foot and then sag slightly back with the weight on the left leg. He will then bow from the waist down while his right arm makes a sweeping gesture in towards the waist.

If he has to kiss the lady's hand he would probably stand with his feet together, bowing from the waist down and bringing her hand up elegantly. Then he will brush the back of her hand lightly with closed lips. Don't kiss her hand with an open, wet mouth – another one of the deadly sins!

If you have not learnt this in your opera school then ask the ballet master of the theatre to show you what to do.

## What to do if things go wrong on stage

The first rule is never to become private. If you stay in your character, you will find that it is quite easy to master an unexpected situation. If you are singing Butterfly and you lose a shoe when you are about to commit suicide, you would obviously do absolutely nothing about it. If you are singing Despina and drop a cup, you obviously simply pick it up.

A case in point    We once saw a student production where four singers were cast as servants. During their scene, a tray with champagne glasses was accidentally dropped. They were so shocked by an incident that had not been rehearsed that they just "froze" and soon after left the stage. The rest of the evening all the protagonists were trying to avoid the glasses on the floor, pretending not to see them. Needless to say the audience was greatly irritated.

## Exercises

Although you should regularly do group exercises with a good teacher, there are nevertheless some exercises that you can do on your own. They will help you train your mental, emotional and physical skills as well as help you develop concentration and discipline.

◆ Stand in front of a mirror and look at your face for at least 15 minutes, observing every contour, shape, line and expression. This is extremely difficult and you will want to stop after one minute. Look yourself straight in the eye and discover your individuality. Tell yourself that there is nobody else on earth with this face and these facial expressions and that you are absolutely unique.

◆ The next time you look into the mirror, start practising facial expressions. Observe which facial muscles you have to use for emotions like anger, joy, confusion, laughter, grief, love and thousands of others. What do you see if you pull down the corners of your mouth? What do you see if you lift your eyebrows, what do you see if you frown? At the beginning you should exaggerate the expressions. When you have done this, then try to add the actual inner feeling to the expression.

◆ Now go away from the mirror and try laughing or crying out loud. Use the panting method as described before. There are many different ways to laugh or cry. You can for instance laugh loudly, quietly, sadistically, hysterically, sarcastically or giggle. You can cry furiously, disappointedly, in pain, anxiously, or joyfully. Try them all. You will be surprised to discover that you will actually start feeling the emotion during the exercise.

◆ Now do the same with anger and hate. To help you feel or express extreme anger, you should use some kind of prop which you can either punch or throw. While you are doing this, say the words "I am furious" or "I hate you" as loudly as possible.

◆ Start observing yourself in everyday life very carefully. What do you see if you catch a sudden glimpse of yourself in a shop window or see a photo or a video of yourself? What does your body language or facial expression tell you? Do you look tired, depressed, lively, joyful, or dynamic? Is there something that you could change in your posture or body language? Is your personality coming across? Are you satisfied with what you see? Analyze yourself critically and objectively!

**179**

◆ As we have already said before, learn to observe other people in everyday life carefully. Then go home and try out the different postures, gestures and facial expressions. To begin with you should exaggerate to establish the feeling in your body memory. Later you can reduce to create a natural expression.

◆ Try miming everyday gestures like combing your hair, putting on your socks or drinking a cup of tea without the actual objects. See if you can remember exactly in every detail how these actions are done.

◆ To train your sensory memory, try and remember what something tastes like. It can be a lemon, a spoonful of vinegar, a sweet piece of chocolate, etc.

◆ Try remembering different noises like a bell ringing, a dog barking, a bird warbling or the brakes of a car screeching.

◆ Read the weather forecast aloud and try out different emotions in your voice. Read it secretly, joyfully, funnily, etc.

◆ If you walk onto the rehearsal stage, feel the dimensions of the space around you. Imagine that the space is much bigger and that you have to project your personality as far as possible into this huge space.

◆ If you have difficulty portraying an aria, practise it at home while washing the dishes or peeling potatoes, thereby making it an integral part of yourself. Then, when you are working with the stage director, you will be free to add or subtract whatever is necessary.

◆ Sing the aria while sitting on a huge inflated rubber ball as used in gymnastic studios. This will help you to bundle your energies and to understand that the interpretation of an aria has to come from the core of your being.

Poise is grounded energy and buoyancy

◆ Read through the other parts and act them out to get a feeling for your relationship with your protagonists.

◆ Train your feeling of balance and buoyancy by standing on an escalator or in a train without holding onto anything.

◆ Do stretching exercises to provide body awareness and flexibility. Just as you warm up the vocal muscles you must

also warm up your body because this is your acting instrument.

* Look and learn all the time. Thinking
that you know everything will make you stagnate.

A great artist never stops learning!

We strongly recommend doing qigong (also called chi kung).
This is an ancient self-healing method from China which
combines controlled breathing, focused mental concentration
and simple movement. In qigong, the mind is the presence of
intention, the movement is the action of intention and the
breath is the flow of intention. The ultimate goal of qigong
is harmonious existence and action in all situations. The
elements that characterize this level of experience include
curiosity, ease in action, clarity of focus and intention, perse-
verance, non-attachment, resilience, openness, creativity, re-
sponsiveness and fluid balance. These are exactly the goals
that a singer-actor should strive for.

Tip

## Last but not least: Personality or charisma

"Charisma is usually assumed to be based on the intuitive,
and is essentially unteachable. But it must consist of external
signs as well as internal magnetism, and these external signs
can be isolated and exercised individually. One of these external signs, for example, is a sense of concentration, of focus
on the task-at-hand that conveys to the audience that the total
being of the performer is involved in the act of performance"
(Wesley Balk, The Complete Singer-Actor).

A young singer-actor may have all the vocal and acting skills
and business sense in the world, but if he is lacking in personality he will have great difficulty achieving his aims.
Personality, or charisma or star quality as it is sometimes
called, cannot be defined, but is something magical that com-
municates itself to an audience on a subliminal level. To be
born with a great personality is a boon in the singing busi-

ness, but it is also something that you can learn by following certain rules.

♦ Wherever you go, even if only into the canteen, walk in with a bounce in your step and a smile on your lips. Look directly at the colleagues and try to communicate energy and radiance.

♦ Learn to walk like a singer. Don't slouch but always keep a posture that radiates confidence and energy.

♦ Focus your intention and concentration on the people around you and stop thinking of your own problems. Learn to look and listen. This will automatically help you project your personality outward.

♦ Dress like a singer. This does not mean being overdressed! But if you dress with a certain flair and elegance it will help you to feel like a singer.

♦ Think of yourself as a larger-than-life personality.

"The final product of one's opera studies should be ... a performer who has good vocal technique *and* who sings with musical sensitivity *and* good diction *and* dramatic understanding *and* who acts well, projects emotion well, moves well *and* who is imaginative and flexible *and*, most of all, who can combine all these skills in a single coordinated act of total music-theater" (Wesley Balk, The Complete Singer-Actor).

## Test your Suitability for the Profession

You have a good voice, musicality and acting talent? But this should be taken for granted. The profession demands much more! Therefore, think very carefully about your decision. The following questionnaire might help. Try to be very objective about yourself. You might also want to ask a good friend to help you with an honest opinion.

| | Yes | No |
|---|---|---|
| ◆ Do you need a regular income to feel safe? | Yes ☐ | No ☐ |
| ◆ Do you have a time-consuming hobby (besides opera)? | Yes ☐ | No ☐ |
| ◆ Do you prefer being at home to travelling? | Yes ☐ | No ☐ |
| ◆ Do you like to have a fixed routine? | Yes ☐ | No ☐ |
| ◆ Are you overweight? | Yes ☐ | No ☐ |
| ◆ Do you hate physical training? | Yes ☐ | No ☐ |
| ◆ Do you have a chronic physical disease? | Yes ☐ | No ☐ |
| ◆ Do you have a mental disease? | Yes ☐ | No ☐ |
| ◆ Do you have a poor memory? | Yes ☐ | No ☐ |
| ◆ Do you pay little attention to your appearance? | Yes ☐ | No ☐ |
| ◆ Do you like being alone rather than in a group of people? | Yes ☐ | No ☐ |
| ◆ Do other professions attract you as much as singing? | Yes ☐ | No ☐ |
| ◆ Do you smoke? | Yes ☐ | No ☐ |
| ◆ Are you undisciplined? | Yes ☐ | No ☐ |
| ◆ Do you like to work alone rather than in a team? | Yes ☐ | No ☐ |
| ◆ Do you hate being criticized? | Yes ☐ | No ☐ |
| ◆ Do you have difficulty pursuing your goal consistently? | Yes ☐ | No ☐ |
| ◆ Are you easily discouraged? | Yes ☐ | No ☐ |
| ◆ Do you often feel listless or depressed? | Yes ☐ | No ☐ |
| ◆ Do you avoid appearing in public rather than enjoying it? | Yes ☐ | No ☐ |
| ◆ Do you get bored repeating your voice exercises regularly? | Yes ☐ | No ☐ |
| ◆ Does competition discourage you? | Yes ☐ | No ☐ |
| ◆ Do you feel stressed quickly? | Yes ☐ | No ☐ |
| ◆ Do you need familiar surroundings to feel well balanced? | Yes ☐ | No ☐ |
| ◆ Do you have a poor knowledge of German? | Yes ☐ | No ☐ |

The more "yes" boxes you have marked, the more problems you will have in becoming an opera singer. For every yes-answer, you should ask yourself whether you could change certain traits or attitudes. If you think it will be possible, do it quickly. If you are not prepared to change, you are not suitable for the profession.

**Elizabeth Miller**
„Summer House", 5 Long Street, London XY00 1ZZ, England
☎ +44 (0)1234 567890    Fax +44 (0)1234 567891
Mobil +44 (0) 123 0987654
eamiller@xyzmail.com

ZBF
Generalagentur
Innere Kanalstr. 69
D 50823 Köln                                          15. Juni 2005

Bewerbung

Sehr geehrte Damen und Herren,

ich bin lyrischer Sopran und suche für die Spielzeit 2006/2007 oder später ein
Engagement an einem Opernhaus in Deutschland.
Ich füge meinen Lebenslauf und meine Repertoireliste bei.
Über einen Termin für ein Vorsingen würde ich mich sehr freuen.

Mit freundlichen Grüßen

*Elizabeth Miller*

Elizabeth Miller

# Appendix

**Elizabeth Miller**

**Sopran**

„Summer House",
5 Long Street,
London XY00 1ZZ, England

☎ +44 (0)1234 567890
Fax +44 (0)1234 567891
Mobil +44 (0) 123 0987654

Email: eamiller@xyzmail.com

**Elizabeth Miller**
„Summer House", 5 Long Street, London XY00 1ZZ, England
☎ +44 (0)1234 567890    Fax +44 (0)1234 567891
Mobil +44 (0) 123 0987654
eamiller@xyzmail.com

## Lebenslauf

Geboren am 10. Juli 1980 in London
1998 Abitur
1987–1993 Mitglied im Kinderchor des Royal Opera House Covent Garden

Musikalische Ausbildung:
1998–2003 Guildhall School of Music and Drama
2003 BMus cum laude
2004 Förderjahr an der Guildhall School of Music and Drama

Wettbewerbe:
2003 2. Preis „Mary Garden International Singing Competition"
2004 Finalistin „Internationaler Hans Gabor Belvedere Gesangswettbewerb"

Meisterkurse:
bei Sarah Walker, Joan Dornemann und Graham Johnson

Weitere Qualifikationen:
1985–1992 Ballettausbildung
1988–1995 Klavierunterricht
1993–1997 Violinunterricht
2002 Grundkurs I und II Italienisch in Siena

Sprachen:
Englisch (fließend)
Italienisch (Grundkenntnisse)
Französisch (Schulkenntnisse)
Deutsch (Großes deutsches Sprachdiplom des Goethe-Instituts)

# Appendix

**Elizabeth Miller**
„Summer House", 5 Long Street, London XY00 1ZZ, England
☎ +44 (0)1234 567890    Fax +44 (0)1234 567891
Mobil +44 (0) 123 0987654
eamiller@xyzmail.com

## Repertoire

**Aufgeführte Partien:**

| Despina | Così fan tutte/Mozart | Hochschulaufführung |
|---|---|---|
| Norina | Don Pasquale/Donizetti (Ausschnitte) | Hochschulaufführung |
| Blonde | Die Entführung aus dem Serail/Mozart | Leeds Youth Opera |

**Vollständig studierte Partien:**

| Oscar | Un ballo in maschera | Verdi |
|---|---|---|
| Zerlina | Don Giovanni | Mozart |
| Lauretta | Gianni Schicchi | Puccini |
| Adele | Die Fledermaus (in Englisch) | J. Strauß |

**Teilweise studierte Partien:**

| Ännchen | Der Freischütz | Weber |
|---|---|---|
| Marzelline | Fidelio | Beethoven |
| Gilda | Rigoletto | Verdi |
| Maria | West Side Story | Bernstein |
| Christel | Der Vogelhändler | Zeller |
| Susanna | Le nozze di Figaro | Mozart |

**Konzertrepertoire:**
Sopranpart in Messen und Oratorien von Mozart, Händel, Fauré und Vivaldi
Lieder von Britten, Elgar, Mozart, Schubert, Schumann und Brahms

## Suggested Audition Arias

The following list has been compiled for the young singer auditioning in Germany for the first time.

Before choosing your audition arias you should be very well informed about the roles that will be expected of you in your *Fach*. Read the German opera magazines to find out which operas are being performed that specific season, listen to recordings and follow the advice of your teacher and musical coach.

But above all, follow your own instincts.

You should know your audition arias so well that you can sing them in your sleep. Never sing an aria that you have not studied with your teacher, your musical coach and your acting coach. You cannot just "sing" an aria – you have to present it with personality and pizzazz!

It goes without saying that you will know the role and not just the aria which you are presenting. You are selling yourself as an opera singer and not as an aria singer.

You should sing arias that come from operas which are regularly performed in German opera houses (remember supply and demand!). You are selling a product that you want the opera director to buy. If you want to sing an aria from an opera that is not often performed, then add it to the bottom of your list, but first offer the arias from roles you will need for your *Fach*.

If you see yourself as a soubrette you must know that there will be no vacancies for this single *Fach* in the Germany of today. You will also have to sing arias of the light lyric or light coloratura *Fach* to improve your chances of getting a job. The same applies to the character alto which is not necessarily seen as a separate *Fach*. Very often the lyric or dramatic mezzo in an opera house has to sing these parts over and above their own roles. Lyric mezzos will have difficulty finding German audition arias. Here it will be acceptable to sing the first scene from *Der Rosenkavalier* and the Olga aria (*Evgeny Onegin*) in German.

We have listed some dramatic categories, but we want to warn all of you with heavy voices that you should not audition the big *Fach* as a beginner. If you offer yourself as a Tosca, Cavaradossi or Filippo, you will find that the German agents and opera directors will not take you seriously, and will prefer you to sing roles of a lighter *Fach*. Even if you sang Tosca or Sieglinde at opera school you should audition with lighter roles such as the Contessa or Agathe.

Another example is Wolfram's scene and aria, "Lied an den Abendstern" from *Tannhäuser*, a wonderfully romantic aria that every young lyric baritone loves to sing. Once you listen to the orchestration and learn the entire role you will soon discover that your voice might not be powerful enough or you might not yet have the physical and mental stamina for this difficult Wagner role. If you cannot see yourself singing the whole role on stage with an orchestra then don't audition with the aria! This is a general rule for all of you out there who think you can sing Butterfly or Don Carlos.

Your list of audition arias must always offer at least one aria by Mozart, one aria in German and one aria in Italian. A French aria or an operetta aria is also a very good idea.

Always sing in the original language, the only exception being the French operettas that are mostly performed in German.

We quote the first lines of arias in our list but it goes without saying that you must always learn the recitative that precedes the aria.

The arias that are usually sung for auditions have been marked with asterisks. The unmarked arias should only be sung if an agent or opera house specifically asks for them or you know that the opera is being performed by the opera house you are singing for. The same applies to the bravura arias which should only be sung if you want to show a particularly virtuose technique.

**Tips**

* Read *The Art of Auditioning* by Anthony Legge.
* Read *Complete Preparation* by Joan Dornemann.
* Read Kloiber: *Handbuch der Oper*, because this is the definitive guide used by all opera houses and agents in Germany.
* Look under www.aria-database.com to find a comprehensive guide to operatic arias.
* In German there are two ways of writing a double s: The ß (the so called long s) like in the name of the operetta composer Johann Strauß and the ss ("double s") like in the name of the opera composer Richard Strauss. It is important for you to know this when writing your repertoire list even if your keyboard does not provide the international alphabet.

The most important arias are marked with an asterisk.

Opera: **Marie:** Er ist so gut, so brav und bieder/Wir armen, armen Mädchen (Der Waffenschmied, Lortzing) ◆ **Marie:** Die Eifersucht ist eine Plage/Lieblich röten sich die Wangen (Zar und Zimmermann, Lortzing) ◆ **Baronin Freimann:** Auf des Lebens raschen Wogen (Der Wildschütz, Lortzing) ◆ **Ännchen:** Kommt ein schlanker Bursch*/Einst träumte meiner sel'gen Base (Der Freischütz, Weber) ◆ **Despina:** In uomini, in soldati*/Una donna a quindici anni* (Così fan tutte, Mozart) ◆ **Zerlina:** Batti, batti o bel Masetto*/Vedrai, carino (Don Giovanni, Mozart) ◆ **Susanna:** Deh vieni, non tardar* (Le nozze di Figaro, Mozart) ◆ **Ilia:** Padre! Germani! Addio!*/Zeffiretti lusinghieri (Idomeneo, Mozart) ◆ **Marzelline:** O wär' ich schon mit dir vereint* (Fidelio, Beethoven) ◆ **Musetta:** Quando me'n vo' (La Bohème, Puccini) ◆ **Lauretta:** O mio babbino caro (Gianni Schicchi, Puccini) ◆ **Sophie:** Ich bin Euer Liebden* (Der Rosenkavalier, R. Strauss)

Operetta: **Adele:** Mein Herr Marquis*/Spiel ich die Unschuld* (Die Fledermaus, J. Strauß) ◆ **Kurfürstin Marie:** Fröhlich Pfalz/Als geblüht der Kirschenbaum (Der Vogelhändler, Zeller) ◆ **Sonja:** Einer wird kommen* (Der Zarewitsch, Lehár) ◆ **Maria Anna Lisa:** Liebe Du Himmel auf Erden* (Paganini, Lehár) ◆ **Valencienne:** Ich bin eine anständige Frau (Die lustige Witwe, Lehár) ◆ **Gabriele:** Grüß dich Gott, du liebes Nesterl (Wiener Blut, J. Strauß) ◆ **Julia:** Strahlender Mond* (Der Vetter aus Dingsda, Künneke) ◆ **Christel:** Ich bin die Christel von der Post* (Der Vogelhändler, Zeller)

*Lyrischer Sopran leicht (light lyric soprano)*

Opera: **Pamina:** Ach, ich fühl's* (Die Zauberflöte, Mozart ) ◆ **La Contessa:** Porgi amor/Dove sono* (Le nozze di Figaro, Mozart) ◆ **Donna Elvira:** Ah fuggi il traditor/Mi tradì* (Don Giovanni, Mozart) ◆ **Micaëla:** Je dis que rien ne m'épouvante* (Carmen, Bizet) ◆ **Antonia:** Elle a fui, la tourterelle (Les contes d'Hoffmann, Offenbach) ◆ **Marguerite:** Que vois-je là? Ah, je ris* (Faust, Gounod) ◆ **Mimi:** Si. Mi chiamano Mimi*/Donde lieta uscì* (La Bohème, Puccini) ◆ **Liù:** Signore ascolta!*/Tu, che di gel sei cinta* (Turandot, Puccini) ◆ **Manon:** In quelle trine morbide/Sola … perduta … abbandonata* (Manon Lescaut, Puccini) ◆ **Nedda:** Stridono lassù (Pagliacci, Leoncavallo) ◆ **Rusalka:** Měsíčku na nebi (Rusalka, Dvořák) ◆ **Mařenka/Marie:** Ten lásky sen, jak krásný byl! [also acceptable in German] (Prodaná Nevěsta/Die verkaufte Braut, Smetana) ◆ **Tatiana:** Ruskai pogibnu [Letter scene; also acceptable in German] (Evgeny Onegin, Tchaikovsky) ◆ **Anne Truelove:** No word from Tom (The Rake's Progress,

*Lyrischer Sopran schwer (heavy lyric or spinto soprano)*

# Appendix

Stravinsky) ◆ **Ellen Orford:** Embroidery in childhood (Peter Grimes, Britten) ◆ **Magda Sorel:** To this we've come (The Consul, Menotti) Operetta: **Giuditta:** Ich weiß es selber nicht* (Giuditta, Lehár) ◆ **Hanna Glawari:** Es lebt' eine Vilja (Die lustige Witwe, Lehár) ◆ **Lisa:** Ich möcht' wieder einmal* (Das Land des Lächelns, Lehár) ◆ **Sylva Varescu:** Heia heia in den Bergen* (Die Csàrdasfürstin, Kálmán) ◆ **Gräfin Mariza:** Hör ich Pusztaklänge* (Gräfin Mariza, Kálmán) ◆ **M. Jeanne Beçu:** Ich schenk' mein Herz (Die Dubarry, Millöcker)

**Lyrischer Koloratur-sopran (lyric coloratura)**

Opera: **Armida:** Vo' far guerra (Rinaldo, Händel) ◆ **Frau Fluth:** Nun eilt herbei (Die lustigen Weiber von Windsor, Nicolai) ◆ **Blonde:** Durch Zärtlichkeit*/Welche Wonne, welche Lust (Die Entführung aus dem Serail, Mozart) ◆ **Marie:** Salut à la France (La fille du régiment, Donizetti) ◆ **Norina:** Quel guardo, il cavaliere* (Don Pasquale, Donizetti) ◆ **Rosina:** Una voce poco fà* (Il Barbiere di Siviglia, Rossini) ◆ **Juliette:** Je veux vivre* (Roméo et Juliette, Gounod) ◆ **Olympia:** Les oiseaux dans la charmille* (Les Contes d'Hoffmann, Offenbach) ◆ **Gilda:** Caro nome* (Rigoletto, Verdi) ◆ **Oscar:** Volta la terrea*/Saper vorreste(Un ballo in maschera, Verdi) ◆ **Zerbinetta:** Großmächtige Prinzessin* [With the usual cut] (Ariadne auf Naxos, R. Strauss) ◆ **Cunegonde:** Glitter and be gay [With the usual cut] (Candide, Bernstein)
Operetta: See light lyric soprano

**Dramatischer Koloraturso pran (dramatic coloratura)**

Opera: **Cleopatra:** Se pietà di me non senti/Piangerò la sorte mia* (Giulio Cesare in Egitto, Händel) ◆ **Konstanze:** Ach, ich liebte, war so glücklich/Martern aller Arten* (Die Entführung aus dem Serail, Mozart) ◆ **Königin der Nacht:** O zittre nicht, mein lieber Sohn*/Der Hölle Rache* (Die Zauberflöte, Mozart) ◆ **Fiordiligi:** Come scoglio* (Così fan tutte, Mozart) ◆ **Vitellia:** Non più di fiori (La clemenza di Tito, Mozart) ◆ **Donna Anna:** Or sai chi l'onore*/Non mi dir, bell'idol mio* (Don Giovanni, Mozart) ◆ **Lucia:** Regnava nel silenzio* (Lucia di Lammermoor, Donizetti) ◆ **Semiramide:** Bel raggio lusinghier* (Semiramide, Rossini) ◆ **Violetta:** Ah, fors' è lui … Sempre libera*/ Addio del passato* (La Traviata, Verdi) ◆ **Lulu:** Wenn sich die Menschen (Lulu, Berg)
Operetta: See heavy lyric soprano

**Jugendlich-dramatischer Sopran (heroic soprano)**

Opera: **Elettra:** D'Oreste, d'Ajace! (Idomeneo, Mozart) ◆ **Agathe:** Wie nahte mir … Leise, leise*/Und ob die Wolke sie verhülle (Der Freischütz, Weber) ◆ **Elisabeth:** Dich teure Halle* (Tannhäuser, Wagner) ◆ **Elsa:** Einsam in trüben Tagen (Lohengrin, Wagner) ◆ **Ariadne:**

Es gibt ein Reich (Ariadne auf Naxos, R. Strauss) ◆ **Leonora:** Tacea la notte placida*/D'amor sull'ali rosee vanne (Il Trovatore, Verdi) ◆ **Amelia:** Ecco l'orrido campo* (Un ballo in maschera, Verdi) ◆ **Elisabetta:** Tu che le vanità (Don Carlo, Verdi) ◆ **Desdemona:** Piangea cantando (Otello, Verdi) ◆ **Cio-Cio-San:** Un bel dì vedremo*/Che tua madre (Madama Butterfly, Puccini) ◆ **Floria Tosca:** Vissi d'arte (Tosca, Puccini)
Operetta: **Rosalinde:** Klänge der Heimat [Csárdás]* (Die Fledermaus, J. Strauß) ◆ **Saffi:** So elend und so treu* (Der Zigeunerbaron, J. Strauß)

Opera: **Ottavia:** Disprezzata regina/Addio Roma (L'incoronazione di Poppea, Monteverdi) ◆ **Penelope:** Di misera regina (Il ritorno d'Ulisse in Patria, Monteverdi) ◆ **Orfeo:** Che farò senza Euridice* (Orfeo ed Euridice, Gluck) ◆ **Giulio Cesare:** Va tacito e nascosto (Giulio Cesare in Egitto, Händel) ◆ **Rinaldo:** Venti, turbini/Or la tomba/Abbrucio, avvampo e fremo (Rinaldo, Händel) ◆ **Sesto:** Svegliatevi nel core/L'angue offeso mai riposa (Giulio Cesare in Egitto, Händel) ◆ **Ariodante:** Dopo notte (Ariodante, Händel) ◆ **Ruggiero:** Verdi prati (Alcina, Händel) ◆ **Serse:** Ombra mai fù (Serse, Händel) ◆ **Romeo:** Deh, tu bell'anima (I Capuleti e i Montecchi, Bellini) ◆ **Arsace:** Ah! Quel giorno ognor rammento (Semiramide, Rossini) ◆ **Tancredi:** Tu che accendi questo cor (Tancredi, Rossini) ◆ **Cherubino:** Non so più*/Voi, che sapete* (Le nozze di Figaro, Mozart) ◆ **Dorabella:** Smanie implacabili* (Così fan tutte, Mozart) ◆ **Sesto:** Parto, parto, ma tu ben mio*/Deh per questo istante solo (La clemenza di Tito, Mozart) ◆ **Idamante:** Il padre adorato* (Idomeneo, Mozart) ◆ **Rosina:** Una voce poco fà* (Il Barbiere di Siviglia, Rossini) ◆ **Isabella:** Cruda sorte!* (L'Italiana in Algeri, Rossini) ◆ **Cenerentola:** Nacqui all'affano e al pianto* (La Cenerentola, Rossini) ◆ **Leonora:** O mio Fernando! [also acceptable in French] (La Favorita, Donizetti) ◆ **Siébel:** Faites-lui mes aveux/Si le bonheur à sourire t'invite (Faust, Gounod) ◆ **Charlotte:** Werther [letter scene]/Va! laisse couleur mes larmes* (Werther, Massenet) ◆ **Olga:** Ya nye spasobna k'grusti tomnoi* [also acceptable in German] (Evgeny Onegin, Tchaikovsky) ◆ **Jeanne d'Arc:** Da chas nastal! [also known as Adieu forêts] (Orleanskaja dewa/Jeanne d'Arc, Tchaikovsky) ◆ **Oktavian:** Wie du warst! Wie du bist!* (Der Rosenkavalier, R. Strauss) ◆ **Komponist:** Seien wir wieder gut!* (Ariadne auf Naxos, R. Strauss)
Operetta: **Orlofsky:** Ich lade gern mir Gäste ein* (Die Fledermaus, J. Strauß) ◆ **Périchole:** Ah! quel diner je viens de faire!* (La Périchole, Offenbach) ◆ **Grand-Duchesse:** Ah! Que j'aime le militaire!

Lyrischer Mezzosopran, auch Koloratur-Mezzosopran (lyric mezzo also mezzo-coloratura)

# Appendix

(La Grand-Duchesse de Gerolstein, Offenbach) ✦ **Manja:** War einmal ein reicher Prasser* (Gräfin Mariza, Kálmán)

**Dramatischer Mezzosopran (dramatic mezzo)**

**Opera: Die Knusperhexe:** Nun Jüngelchen, ergötze dein Züngelchen (Hänsel und Gretel, Humperdinck) ✦ **Carmen:** L'amour est un oiseau rebelle*/Près de remparts de Séville* (Carmen, Bizet) ✦ **Eboli:** Nei giardin del bello/O don fatale* (Don Carlo, Verdi) ✦ **Azucena:** Condotta ell'era in ceppi*/Stride la vampa (Il Trovatore, Verdi) ✦ **Laura:** Stella del marinar!* (La Gioconda, Ponchielli) ✦ **Waltraute:** Höre mit Sinn, was ich sage! (Götterdämmerung, Wagner) ✦ **Fricka:** So ist es denn aus (Die Walküre, Wagner) ✦ **Baba the Turk:** As I was saying/Scorned! Abused! Neglected!* (The Rake's Progress, Stravinsky)
**Operetta:** See character alto

**Spielalt (character alto)**

**Opera: Arnalta:** Oggi, oggi sarà Poppea (L'incoronazione di Poppea, Monteverdi) ✦ **Berta:** Il vecchietto cerca moglie* (Il Barbiere di Siviglia, Rossini) ✦ **Fidalma:** È vero che in casa (Il matrimonio segreto, Cimarosa) ✦ **Frugola:** Se tu sapessi (Il tabarro, Puccini) ✦ **Irmentraut:** Welt du kannst mir nicht gefallen* (Der Waffenschmied, Lortzing) ✦ **Magdalena:** O holde Jugendtage [for chorus audition] (Der Evangelimann, Kienzl)
**Operetta: Gräfin Kokozeff:** Alles mit der Ruhe* (Der Graf von Luxemburg, Lehár) ✦ **Boulotte:** In unserm Dorf (Barbe-Bleu/*Blaubart*, Offenbach)

**Dramatischer Alt (dramatic alto)**

**Opera: Ericlea:** Ericlea, chè vuoi far (Il ritorno d'Ulisse in Patria, Monteverdi) ✦ **Cornelia:** Priva son d'ogni conforto* (Giulio Cesare in Egitto, Händel) ✦ **Argante:** Sibillar gli angui d'Aletto (Rinaldo, Händel) ✦ **Dalila:** Mon cœur s'ouvre à ta voix*/Amour! Viens aider ma faiblesse! (Samson et Dalila, Saint-Saëns) ✦ **Ulrica:** Re dell'abisso, affrettati* (Un ballo in maschera, Verdi) ✦ **Gäa:** Dein Zagen kenn ich* (Daphne, R. Strauss) ✦ **Erda:** Weiche, Wotan, weiche!* (Das Rheingold, Wagner)

**Kontratenor (counter tenor or male alto)**

**Opera: Orfeo:** Che farò senza Euridice (Orfeo ed Euridice, Gluck) ✦ **Arsace:** Furibondo spira il vento (Partenope, Händel) ✦ **Giulio Cesare:** Va tacito e nascosto* (Giulio Cesare in Egitto, Händel) ✦ **Orlando:** Fammi combattere* (Orlando, Händel) ✦ **Ariodante:** Dopo notte* (Ariodante, Händel) ✦ **Serse:** Ombra mai fù (Serse, Händel) ✦ **Arsemene:** Non so che sia la speme/Si, la voglio (Serse, Händel) ✦ **Farnace:** Va, l'error mio palesa* (Mitridate, Rè di Ponto, Mozart) ✦

**Oberon:** I know a bank (A midsummer night's dream, Britten) ◆
**Edgar:** Habe ich mein Leben (Lear, Reimann)
**Operetta: Orlofsky:** Ich lade gern mir Gäste ein (Die Fledermaus, J. Strauß)

**Opera: Georg:** Man wird ja einmal nur geboren (Der Waffenschmied, Lortzing) ◆ **Die Knusperhexe:** Nun Jüngelchen, ergötze dein Züngelchen (Hänsel und Gretel, Humperdinck) ◆ **Pedrillo:** Frisch zum Kampfe!*/Im Mohrenland gefangen war (Die Entführung aus dem Serail, Mozart) ◆ **Monostatos:** Alles fühlt der Liebe Freuden* (Die Zauberflöte, Mozart) ◆ **Beppo:** O Colombina, il tenero fido (I Pagliacci, Leoncavallo) ◆ **Wenzel/Vašek:** To, to me vhlavĕleží [also acceptable in German] (Prodanà Nevĕsta/Die verkaufte Braut, Smetana) ◆ **David:** Mein Herr, der Singer Meisterschlag* (Die Meistersinger von Nürnberg, Wagner)
**Operetta: Adam:** Grüß euch Gott, alle miteinander*/Schenkt man sich Rosen*/Wie mei Ahn'l zwanzig Jahr (Der Vogelhändler, Zeller) ◆ **Leopold:** Es muss was Wunderbares sein* (Im weißen Rössl, Benatzky) ◆ **Toni:** Wenn ich in den Zirkus gehe (Die Zirkusprinzessin, Kálmán)

**Spieltenor (tenor buffo)**

**Opera: Orfeo:** Possente spirto (La favola d'Orfeo, Monteverdi) ◆ **Lurcanio:** Il tuo sangue (Ariodante, Händel) ◆ **Grimoaldo:** Tuo drudo è mio rivale/Prigioniera (Rodelinda, Händel) ◆ **Bertarido:** Vivi tiranno (Rodelinda, Händel) ◆ **Bajazete:** Ciel e terra (Tamerlano, Händel) ◆ **Lyonel:** Ach! So fromm, ach so traut (Martha, Flotow) ◆ **Fenton:** Horch die Lerche singt* (Die lustigen Weiber von Windsor, Nicolai) ◆ **Chateauneuf:** Lebe wohl, mein flandrisch Mädchen (Zar und Zimmermann, Lortzing) ◆ **Belmonte:** Hier soll ich dich denn sehen/Konstanze, dich wiederzusehen*/Wenn der Freude Tränen/Ich baue ganz (Die Entführung aus dem Serail, Mozart) ◆ **Ferrando:** Un'aura amorosa*/Tradito, schernito dal perfido cor (Così fan tutte, Mozart) ◆ **Don Ottavio:** Dalla sua pace*/Il mio tesoro intanto* (Don Giovanni, Mozart) ◆ **Tamino:** Dies Bildnis* (Die Zauberflöte, Mozart) ◆ **Almaviva:** Ecco ridente in cielo* (Il Barbiere di Siiglia, Rossini) ◆ **Nemorino:** Una furtiva lagrima* (L'elisir d'amore, Donizetti) ◆ **Tonio:** Ah! mes amis. Pour mon âme* [For tenors with a great top!] (La fille du régiment, Donizetti) ◆ **Lenski:** Kuda, kuda* [also acceptable in German] (Evgeny Onegin, Tchaikovsky) ◆ **Tom Rakewell:** Here I stand/Love too frequently (The Rake's Progress, Stravinsky)
**Operetta: Leutnant Niki:** Leise, ganz leise (Ein Walzertraum, O. Straus) ◆ **Pâris:** Au mont Ida, trois Déesses (La belle Hélène,

**Lyrischer Tenor leicht (light lyric tenor)**

# Appendix

Offenbach) ✦ **Der Zarewitsch:** Allein, wieder allein ... Es steht ein Soldat\*/Hab nur dich allein (Der Zarewitsch, Lehár) ✦ **Paganini:** Gern hab' ich die Frau'n\* (Paganini, Lehár) ✦ **Rossillon:** Wie eine Rosenknospe (Die lustige Witwe, Lehár) ✦ **Mister X:** Zwei Märchenaugen\* (Die Zirkusprinzessin, Kálmán) ✦ **Symon:** Ich knüpfte manche zarte Bande/Ich hab kein Geld, bin vogelfrei (Der Bettelstudent, Millöcker) ✦ **Caramello:** Komm in die Gondel\* (Eine Nacht in Venedig, J. Strauß)

**Lyrischer Tenor schwer (heavy lyric or spinto tenor)**

**Opera: Idomeneo:** Fuor del mar\* (Idomeneo, Mozart) ✦ **Tito:** Se all' impero, amici Dei!\* (La clemenza di Tito, Mozart) ✦ **Max:** Nein länger trag ich nicht die Qualen ... Durch die Wälder (Der Freischütz, Weber) ✦ **Hans/Jeník:** Jak možná věřit\* [also acceptable in German] (Prodaná Nevěsta/Die verkaufte Braut, Smetana) ✦ **Roméo:** Ah, lève-toi, soleil! (Roméo et Juliette, Gounod) ✦ **Il Duca:** Questa o quella\*/Parmi veder le lagrime/La donna è mobile\* (Rigoletto, Verdi) ✦ **Alfredo:** De' miei bollenti spiriti [with cabaletta] (La Traviata, Verdi) ✦ **Riccardo:** Ma se m'è forza perderti\* (Un ballo in maschera, Verdi) ✦ **Macduff:** Ah, la paterna mano\* (Macbeth, Verdi) ✦ **Manrico:** Ah sì, ben mio\*/Di quella pira\* (Il Trovatore, Verdi) ✦ **Don Carlo:** Io l'ho perduta (Il Trovatore, Verdi) ✦ **Rodolfo:** Che gelida manina\* (La Bohème, Puccini) ✦ **Des Grieux:** Donna non vidi mai\* (Manon Lescaut, Puccini) ✦ **Edgardo:** Fra poco a me ricovero\* (Lucia di Lammermoor, Donizetti) ✦ **Don José:** La fleur que tu m'avais jetée\* (Carmen, Bizet) ✦ **Werther:** Je ne sais si je veille\*/Pourquoi me réveiller (Werther, Massenet) ✦ **Faust:** Salut! demeure chaste et pure\* (Faust, Gounod) ✦ **Hoffmann:** Il était une fois (Les contes d'Hoffmann, Offenbach)

**Operetta: Graf Tassilo:** Komm Zigány\*/Grüß mir die süßen (Gräfin Mariza, Kálmán) ✦ **Barinkay:** Als flotter Geist\* (Der Zigeunerbaron, J. Strauß) ✦ **Prinz Sou-Chong:** Von Apfelblüten einen Kranz/Dein ist mein ganzes Herz\*/Immer nur lächeln (Das Land des Lächelns, Lehár) ✦ **Octavio:** Freunde, das Leben ist lebenswert\* (Giuditta, Lehár)

**Jugendlicher Heldentenor (youthful heroic tenor)**

**Opera: Canio:** Vesti la giubba\* (I Pagliacci, Leoncavallo) ✦ **Cavaradossi:** Recondita armonia\*/E lucevan le stelle\* (Tosca, Puccini) ✦ **Turiddu:** Mamma, quel vino è generoso (Cavalleria rusticana, Mascagni) ✦ **Erik:** Willst jenes Tags\* (Der fliegende Holländer, Wagner) ✦ **Peter Grimes:** Now the great bear/Go there!\* (Peter Grimes, Britten)

**Operetta:** See heavy lyric tenor

Opera: **Ulisse:** Dormo ancora (Il ritorno d'Ulisse, Monteverdi) ◆ **Graf v. Eberbach:** Heiterkeit und Fröhlichkeit* (Der Wildschütz, Lortzing) ◆ **Graf v. Liebenau:** Willst du mich der Verzweiflung (Der Waffenschmied, Lortzing) ◆ **Papageno:** Der Vogelfänger bin ich ja*/Ein Mädchen oder Weibchen* (Die Zauberflöte, Mozart) ◆ **Guglielmo:** Rivolgete a lui lo sguardo* [mostly cut, but a good audition aria]/Donne mie, la fate a tanti* (Così fan tutte, Mozart) ◆ **Valentin:** Avant de quitter ces lieux ... O sainte médaille* (Faust, Gounod) ◆ **Belcore:** Come Paride vezzoso (L'elisir d'amore, Donizetti) ◆ **Malatesta:** Bella siccome un angelo* (Don Pasquale, Donizetti) ◆ **Dandini:** Come un'ape ne'giorni d'aprile (La Cenerentola, Rossini) ◆ **Fritz:** Mein Sehnen, mein Wähnen (Die tote Stadt, Korngold)
Operetta: **Graf Danilo:** O Vaterland, du machst bei Tag* (Die lustige Witwe, Lehár) ◆ **Erminio:** Dunkelrote Rosen bring' ich (Gasparone, Millöcker) ◆ **Graf Homonay:** Her die Hand, es muss ja sein* (Der Zigeunerbaron, J. Strauß) ◆ **Graf Boni:** Ganz ohne Weiber* (Die Csárdásfürstin, Kálmán)

**Lyrischer Bariton (lyric baritone)**

Opera: **Peter I.:** Sonst spielt' ich mit Zepter (Zar und Zimmermann, Lortzing) ◆ **Il Conte Almaviva:** Vedrò, mentr'io sospiro* (Le nozze di Figaro, Mozart) ◆ **Don Giovanni:** Fin ch'han dal vino/Deh, vieni alla finestra (Don Giovanni, Mozart) ◆ **Dapertutto:** Scintille diamant* (Les contes d'Hoffmann, Offenbach) ◆ **Escamillo:** Votre toast, je peux vous le rendre* (Carmen, Bizet) ◆ **Figaro:** Largo al factotum* (Il Barbiere di Siviglia, Rossini) ◆ **Enrico:** Cruda, funesta smania (Lucia di Lammermoor, Donizetti) ◆ **Giorgio Germont:** Di Provenza il mar (La Traviata, Verdi) ◆ **Ford:** È sogno o realtà?* (Falstaff, Verdi) ◆ **Renato:** Eri tu* (Un ballo in maschera, Verdi) ◆ **Conte di Luna:** Il balen del suo sorriso* (Il Trovatore, Verdi) ◆ **Rigoletto:** Cortigiani, vil razza* (Rigoletto, Verdi) ◆ **Iago:** Credo in un Dio crudel* (Otello, Verdi) ◆ **Rodrigo:** Per me giunto è il dì supremo* (Don Carlo, Verdi) ◆ **Jeletzkij:** Ya vas lyublyu (Pikowaja dama, Tchaikovsky) ◆ **Evgeny Onegin:** Ví mne pisali/Uzhel ta samaja Tatiana (Arioso)* [also acceptable in German] (Evgeny Onegin, Tchaikovsky) ◆ **Wolfram:** Wie Todesahnung ... O du mein holder Abendstern (Tannhäuser, Wagner) ◆ **Billy Budd:** Look! Through the port comes the moonshine astray! (Billy Budd, Britten)
Operetta: See lyric baritone

**Kavalierbariton (heavy lyric baritone)**

Opera: **Baculus:** Fünftausend Taler!* (Der Wildschütz, Lortzing) ◆ **Hans Stadinger:** Auch ich war ein Jüngling (Der Waffenschmied, Lortzing) ◆ **Van Bett:** O sancta justitia! (Zar und Zimmermann,

**Spielbass (bass buffo)**

Lortzing) ♦ **Bartolo:** La vendetta* (Le nozze di Figaro, Mozart) ♦ **Leporello:** Madamina!* (Don Giovanni, Mozart) ♦ **Bartolo:** A un dottor* (Il Barbiere di Siviglia, Rossini) ♦ **Don Pasquale:** Ah! un foco insolito* (Don Pasquale, Donizetti)
**Operetta: General Bumm:** A cheval sur la discipline* (La Grande Duchesse de Gérolstein, Offenbach) ♦ **Zsupan:** Ja, das Schreiben und das Lesen* (Der Zigeunerbaron, J. Strauß) ♦ **Fürst Basil:** Kam ein Falter leicht geflattert (Der Graf von Luxemburg, Lehár) ♦ **Oberst Ollendorf:** Und da soll man noch galant sein* [D-major] (Der Bettelstudent, Millöcker) ♦ **Nasoni:** Auch ich war einst ein junger Mann* (Gasparone, Millöcker)

**Bassbariton, auch Heldenbariton (bass-baritone)**

**Opera: Argante:** Sibillar gl'angui d'Aletto (Rinaldo, Händel) ♦ **Figaro:** Non più andrai*/Se vuol ballare/Aprite un po' quegl'occhi* (Le nozze di Figaro, Mozart) ♦ **Alidoro:** Là nel ciel nell'arcano profondo (La Cenerentola, Rossini) ♦ **Sir John Falstaff:** L'onore! Ladri!* (Falstaff, Verdi) ♦ **Tonio:** Si può?* (Pagliacci, Leoncavallo) ♦ **Mephistopheles:** Le veau d'or*/Vous qui faites l'endormie (Faust, Gounod)
**Operetta:** See bass buffo

**Bass (heavy bass or basso profondo)**

**Opera: Seneca:** Ecco, la sconsolata donna (L'íncoronazione di Poppea, Monteverdi) ♦ **Kaspar:** Schweig, schweig* (Der Freischütz, Weber) ♦ **Sir John Falstaff:** Als Büblein klein (Die lustigen Weiber von Windsor, Nicolai) ♦ **Sarastro:** O Isis und Osiris*/In diesen heil'gen Hallen* (Die Zauberflöte, Mozart) ♦ **Osmin:** Wer ein Liebchen hat gefunden/Solche hergelaufne Laffen*/Ha! Wie will ich triumphieren* (Die Entführung aus dem Serail, Mozart) ♦ **Rocco:** Hat man nicht auch Gold (Fidelio, Beethoven) ♦ **Basilio:** La calunnia* (Il Barbiere di Siviglia, Rossini) ♦ **Colline:** Vecchia zimarra* (La Bohème, Puccini) ♦ **Banco:** Come dal ciel precipita* (Macbeth, Verdi) ♦ **Filippo:** Ella giammai m'amò* (Don Carlo, Verdi) ♦ **Fiesco:** Il lacerato spirito* (Simon Boccanegra, Verdi) ♦ **Fürst Gremin:** Lyubvi vse vozrasti pakorni* [also acceptable in German] (Evgeny Onegin, Tchaikovsky) ♦ **Daland:** Mögst du mein Kind (Der fliegende Holländer, Wagner)
**Operetta:** see bass buffo

# Bibliography

Ardoin, John: Callas at Juilliard. The Master Classes, New York: Knopf, 1987

Balk, H. Wesley: The Complete Singer-Actor. Training for Music Theater, Minneapolis: University of Minnesota Press, [3]1992

Balk, H. Wesley: Performing Power. A new Approach for the Singer-Actor, Minneapolis: University of Minnesota Press, 1985

Balk, H. Wesley: The Radiant Performer. The Spiral Path to Performing Power, Minneapolis: University of Minnesota Press, 1991

Dornemann, Joan: Complete Preparation. A Guide to Auditioning for Opera, New York: Excalibur Publications, 1992

Green, Barry and W. Timothy Gallwey: The Inner Game of Music, Garden City, NY: Anchor Press, 1986

Helfgot, Daniel, and William O. Beeman: The Third Line. The Opera Performer as Interpreter, New York: Schirmer Books, 1993

Hemsley, Thomas: Singing and Imagination, New York: Oxford University Press, 1998

Hines, Jerome: Great Singers on Great Singing, New York: Limelight, [6]1992

Lamperti, Giovanni B., and William E. Brown: Vocal Wisdom, New York: Crescendo, 1957

Legge, Anthony: The Art of Auditioning, revised and updated edition, London: Peters, 2001

McKinney, James C.: The Diagnosis and Correction of Vocal Faults, Nashville, TN: Broadman Press, 1982

Ristad, Eloise: A Soprano on Her Head, Moab, UT: Real People Press, 1982

Singher, Martial: An Interpretive Guide to Operatic Arias. A Handbook for Singers, Coaches, Teachers, and Students, University Park: Pennsylvania State University Press, 1983

Adams, David: A Handbook of Diction for Singers. Italian, German, French, New York: Oxford University Press, 1999

Barber, Josephine: German for Musicians, London: Faber Music, 1985

Bates, Brian: The Way of the Actor, Boston, MA: Shambhala, 1988

Boldrey, Richard: Guide to Operatic Roles and Arias, Dallas, TX: PST-Inc., 1994

Strongly recommended

Recommended

# Appendix

Bourne, Joyce: Who's who in Opera. A Guide to Opera Characters, Oxford: Oxford University Press, 1999

Brook, Peter: The Empty Space, New York: Simon and Schuster, 1996

Brook, Peter: The Open Door. Thoughts on Acting and Theatre, New York: Anchor Books, 2005

Bunch, Meribeth: Dynamics of the Singing Voice, New York: Springer, 1982

Clark, Mark Ross, and Lynn V. Clark: Singing, Acting, and Movement in Opera. A Guide to Singer-getics, Bloomington: Indiana University Press, 2002

Coffin, Berton, Werner Singer and Pierre Delattre: Word-by-word Translations of Songs and Arias, Metuchen, NJ: Scarecrow Press, 1966–72

Cohen, Kenneth S.: The Way of Qigong, New York: Random House International, 1999

Colorni, Evelina: Singers' Italian. A Manual of Diction and Phonetics, New York: Schirmer Books, 1970

Donald, Olson: Germany for Dummies, New York: Wiley, [2]2005

Douglas, Nigel: Legendary Voices, New York: Limelight, 1995

Douglas, Nigel: More Legendary Voices, New York: Limelight, 1995

Edwards, Geoffrey: The Verdi Baritone. Studies in the Development of Dramatic Character, Bloomington: Indiana University Press, 1994

Edwards, Geoffrey, and Ryan Edwards: Verdi and Puccini Heroines. Dramatic Characterization in Great Soprano Roles, Lanham, MD: Scarecrow Press, 2001

Fleming, Renee: The Inner Voice. The Making of a Singer, New York: Viking, 2004

Flippo, Hyde: The German Way. Aspects of Behavior, Attitudes, and Customs in the German-speaking World, Lincolnwood, IL: Passport Books, 1999

Flippo, Hyde: When in Germany, Do as the Germans Do, Chicago: McGraw-Hill, 2002

Goldovsky, Boris: Bringing Opera to Life. Operatic Acting and Stage Direction, New York: Meredith Corp., 1968

Goldovsky, Boris, and Arthur Schoep: Bringing Soprano Arias to Life, Metuchen, NJ: Scarecrow Press, 1990

Greene, Margaret C. L.: The Voice and its Disorders, Philadelphia, PA: Lippincott, 1975

Grubb, Thomas: Singing in French. A Manual of French Diction and French Vocal Repertoire, New York: Schirmer Books, 1979

Hagen, Uta: A Challenge for the Actor, New York: Scribner's, 1991

Hagen, Uta: Respect for Acting, New York: Macmillan, 1973

Jakoby, Richard, and Egon Kraus: Studying Music in Germany. Music, Music Education, Musicology, Mainz/New York: Schott, [8]2002

Jefferies, William McK.: Safe uses of cortisol, Springfield, IL: Thomas, 1996

Jones, Frank P.: Body Awareness in Action: A Study of the Alexander Technique, revised edition New York: Schocken Books, 1979

Kirkpatrick, Carol: Aria Ready, www.ariaredy.net, 2003

Kloiber, Rudolf, Wulf Konold and Robert Maschka: Handbuch der Oper, erweiterte und aktualisierte Neuauflage, Kassel/ München: Bärenreiter/Deutscher Taschenbuch Verlag, [9]2002

Klotz, Volker: Operette. Porträt und Handbuch einer unerhörten Kunst, erweiterte und aktualisierte Auflage, Kassel: Bärenreiter, 2004

Lenton, Sarah: Backstage at the Opera, London: Robson, 1998

Matheopoulos, Helena: Bravo. The World's Great Male Singers Discuss their Roles, London: Gollancz, 1989

Matheopoulos, Helena: Diva. Great Sopranos and Mezzos Discuss their Art, London: Gollancz, 1991

Matheopoulos, Helena: Diva – The New Generation. The Sopranos and Mezzos of the Decade Discuss their Roles, London: Little, Brown, 1998

Matheopoulos, Helena: The Great Tenors. From Caruso to the Present, London: Laurence King, 1999

Miller, Jonathan: Acting in Opera. The 60 minute BBC Master Class, Video

Miller, Richard: On the Art of Singing, New York: Oxford University Press, 1996

Miller, Richard: The Structure of Singing, New York: Schirmer Books, 1986

Miller, Richard: Training Tenor Voices, New York: Schirmer Books, 1993

Nelson, Samuel H., and Elizabeth Blades-Zeller: Singing with your Whole Self. The Feldenkrais Method and Voice, Lanham, MD: Scarecrow Press, 2002

Nilsson, Birgit: La Nilsson. Mein Leben für die Oper, Frankfurt/ Main: Krüger [3]1997

Odom, William, and Benno Schollum: German for Singers. A Textbook of Diction and Phonetics, New York: Schirmer Books, 1997

# Appendix

Penrod, James: Movement for the Performing Artist, Palo Alto, CA: National Press Books, 1974

Piatak, Jean, and Regina Avrashov: Russian Songs and Arias. Phonetic Readings, Word-by-word Translations, and a Concise Guide to Russian Diction, Dallas, TX: PST-Inc., 1991

Ramacharaka, Yogi: The Hindu-Yogi Science of Breath, London: Fowler, [22]1960

Reid, Cornelius L.: A Dictionary of Vocal Terminology, New York: Patelson Music House, 1983

Rosenthal, Harold, and John H. Warrack: The Concise Oxford Dictionary of Opera, London: Oxford University Press, [2]1979

Scholz, Dieter D.: Mythos Primadonna. 25 Diven widerlegen ein Klischee, Berlin: Parthas, 1999

Stanislavski, Constantin, and Pavel Rumyantsev: Stanislavski on Opera, New York: Routledge, 1998

Stapp, Marcie: The Singers' Guide to Languages, revised edition, San Francisco: Teddy's Music Press, 1996

Stemple, Joseph C.: Clinical Voice Pathology, Toronto: Merrill Publ., 1984

Strasberg, Lee: A Dream of Passion, London: Methuen, 1989

Vennard, William: Singing – the Mechanism and the Technic, New York: C. Fischer, [5]1968

Wall, Joan: Diction for Singers. A Concise Reference for English, Italian, Latin, German, French and Spanish pronunciation, Dallas, TX: PST-Inc., 1990

Wall, Joan: International Phonetic Alphabet for Singers. A Manual for English and Foreign Language Diction, Dallas, TX: PST-Inc., 1989

## Periodicals

Die Bühnengenossenschaft, Hamburg: Genossenschaft Deutscher Bühnenangehöriger

Classical Singer, Draper, UT: Classical Publications Inc.

Deutsches Bühnenjahrbuch, Hamburg: Verlag der Bühnenschriften-Vertriebs-Gesellschaft

Neue Musikzeitung, Regensburg: ConBrio Verlagsgesellschaft

Oper und Tanz, Regensburg: ConBrio Verlagsgesellschaft

Das Opernglas, Hamburg: Opernglas Verlagsgesellschaft

Opernwelt. Das Internationale Opernmagazin, Berlin: Friedrich Verlag

Orpheus, Berlin: Neue Gesellschaft für Musikinformation

PAYE: Performing Arts Yearbook for Europe, London: Arts Publ. International

# Glossary

English – German

act (partition of opera)  der Akt
act (to)  schauspielern
actor  der Schauspieler
actress  die Schauspielerin
ad-hoc chorus  der Extrachor
announcement  die Ansage, die Durchsage
applause  der Beifall, der Applaus
apron (part of stage)  die Vorbühne
artistic administration  das Betriebsbüro
  abbr. KBB
audience  das Publikum, die Zuschauer pl
audition  das Vorsingen
audition (to)  vorsingen
audition date or time  der Vorsingtermin
back cloth (backdrop)  der Prospekt
beginner  der Anfänger/die Anfängerin m/f
blocking rehearsal  die Stellprobe
bow  die Verbeugung
box office  die Theaterkasse
carpenter  der Tischler/die Tischlerin m/f
carpenter's shop  die Tischlerei, die Möbelabteilung
cast  die Besetzung
character (in the sense of "role")  die Figur
chorus  der Chor
chorus master  der Chordirektor
chorus mistress  die Chordirektorin
chorus office  das Chorbüro
company  das Ensemble
complimentary ticket  die Freikarte
conductor  der Dirigent/die Dirigentin m/f
contract  der Vertrag
costume  das Kostüm
costume department  die Schneiderei, die
  Kostümabteilung

costume designer  der Kostümbildner/die
  Kostümbildnerin m/f
costume fitting  die Kostümprobe
cue  das Stichwort
curriculum vitae (CV)  der Lebenslauf
curtain call  die Applausordnung, die Verbeugung
curtain  der Vorhang
curtsy  die Verbeugung
cyclorama  der Rundhorizont
dagger  der Dolch
daily allowance  die Spesen pl, das Tagegeld
décor  das Bühnenbild
dresser  der Garderobier/die Garderobiere
  m/f
dressing-room  die Garderobe
elevator  der Aufzug, der Fahrstuhl, der Lift
expression  der Ausdruck
extra chorus  der Extrachor
fan (admirer)  der Verehrer/die Verehrerin
  m/f, der Fan
fan (costume prop)  der Fächer
fan (for cooling)  der Ventilator
fee  die Gage, das Honorar
final dress rehearsal  die Generalprobe
financial manager  der Verwaltungsdirektor/
  die Verwaltungsdirektorin m/f
fire curtain  der eiserne Vorhang
flies  der Schnürboden
fluff your lines (to)  schmeißen
fly gallery  die Arbeitsgalerie
fly-bar  die Zugstange
follow-spot  der Verfolgungsscheinwerfer,
  der Verfolger
guest (to)  gastieren

# Appendix

**guest appearance** das Gastspiel, der Gastauftritt

**guest contract** der Gastvertrag

**hatch** die Luke

**head of administration** der Verwaltungsdirektor/die Verwaltungsdirektorin *m/f*

**head of artistic administration** der Betriebsbüroleiter/die Betriebsbüroleiterin *m/f*

**head of musical staff** der Studienleiter/die Studienleiterin *m/f*

**houselights** die Saalbeleuchtung

**incidental music (played backstage)** die Bühnenmusik

**intercom** die Lautsprecheranlage

**intermission** die Pause

**interpret (to)** darstellen, gestalten

**interpretation** die Darstellung

**interval** die Pause

**laryngologist** der Phoniater/die Phoniaterin, der Stimmarzt/die Stimmärztin *m/f*

**lift** der Aufzug, der Fahrstuhl, der Lift

**lift (movable section of stage)** die Versenkung

**lighting** die Beleuchtung

**lighting technician** der Beleuchter/die Beleuchterin *m/f*

**loudspeakers** die Lautsprecheranlage

**make up (to)** schminken

**make-up** die Maske, die Schminke

**make-up man** der Maskenbildner

**make-up room** die Maske

**make-up woman** die Maskenbildnerin

**music coach** der Korrepetitor/die Korrepetitorin, der Repetitor/die Repetitorin *m/f*

**music director** der Generalmusikdirektor/die Generalmusikdirektorin *abbr.* GMD *m/f*

**music room** das Musikzimmer

**music school** die Musikhochschule

**music stand** das Notenpult

**no smoking** Rauchen verboten

**nodules** die Stimmknötchen *pl*

**opening night** die Premiere

**opera director** der Intendant/die Intendantin *m/f*

**opera house** das Opernhaus

**opera season** die Spielzeit

**orchestra** das Orchester

**orchestra dress rehearsal** die Hauptprobe

**orchestra pit** der Orchestergraben

**orchestra rehearsal** die Orchesterprobe

**orchestral score** die Partitur

**pay** die Bezahlung

**per diem** die Spesen *pl*, das Tagegeld

**performance** die Aufführung, die Vorstellung

**performer** der Darsteller/die Darstellerin *m/f*

**piano dress rehearsal** die Klavierhauptprobe

**piano score** der Klavierauszug

**portray (to)** gestalten, darstellen

**prompt (to)** soufflieren

**prompt/prompter** der Souffleur/die Souffleuse *m/f*

**prompter's box** der Souffleurkasten

**prop master** der Requisiteur

**prop mistress** die Requisiteurin

**properties (props)** die Requisiten *pl*

**rake (slant of stage floor)** die Schräge

**rapier** der Degen

**recording** die Aufnahme

**rehearsal** die Probe

**rehearsal hall** der Probesaal

**rehearsal room** das Probenzimmer

**rehearsal schedule** der Probenplan

**rehearsal stage** die Probebühne

**rehearse (to)** proben

**repertoire** das Repertoire

**repertory** der Spielplan

**résumé** der Lebenslauf

**revival production** die Wiederaufnahme

**revolving stage** die Drehbühne

**role** die Rolle

**safety curtain** der eiserne Vorhang

**safety pin** die Sicherheitsnadel
**salary** die Gage, das Gehalt
**scene (partition of opera)** das Bild, die Szene
**scene-change** der Szenenwechsel, die Verwandlung
**scenery** das Bühnenbild
**scenic/set designer** der Bühnenbildner/die Bühnenbildnerin *m/f*
**seamstress** die Schneiderin
**second cast** die Zweitbesetzung
**set change** der Umbau
**set** die Ausstattung, die Dekoration
**singer** der Sänger/die Sängerin *m/f*
**singing teacher** der Gesangslehrer/die Gesangslehrerin *m/f*
**sound** der Ton
**sound technician** der Tontechniker/die Tontechnikerin *m/f*
**spotlight** der Scheinwerfer
**stage** die Bühne
**stage director** der Regisseur/die Regisseurin *m/f*
**stage director's assistant** der Regieassistent/die Regieassistentin *m/f*
**stage door** der Bühneneingang, die Pforte
**stage door man** der Bühnenpförtner, der Pförtner
**stage door woman** die Bühnenpförtnerin, die Pförtnerin
**stage fright** das Lampenfieber
**stage hand** der Bühnenarbeiter/die Bühnenarbeiterin *m/f*

**stage left** Bühne links
**stage manager** der Inspizient/die Inspizientin *m/f*
**stage manager's call** der Einruf
**stage manager's desk** das Inspizientenpult
**stage orchestral rehearsal** die Bühnenorchesterprobe *abbr.* BO
**stage rehearsal** die Bühnenprobe
**stage right** Bühne rechts
**stage trap door** die Bodenklappe, die Versenkungsklappe
**staging rehearsal** die szenische Probe
**super** der Statist/die Statistin *m/f*
**supers** die Statisterie
**sword** das Schwert
**tailor** der Schneider
**tannoy** die Lautsprecheranlage
**ticket** die Eintrittskarte
**understudy** der/die Mitstudierende *m/f*
**understudy (to)** mitstudieren
**vocal folds** die Stimmlippen *pl*
**vocal score** der Klavierauszug
**voice** die Stimme
**voice teacher** der Gesangslehrer/die Gesangslehrerin *m/f*
**voice type** das Fach, das Stimmfach
**voice type change** der Fachwechsel
**walk-on** der Statist/die Statistin *m/f*
**wig** die Perücke
**wig-maker** der Perückenmacher/die Perückenmacherin *m/f*
**wings** die Seitenbühne, die Kulisse

# Appendix

German – English

**Akt, der** act (partition of opera)
**Ansage, die** announcement
**Applaus, der** applause
**Applausordnung, die** curtain call
**Arbeitsgalerie, die** fly gallery
**Aufführung, die** performance
**Aufnahme, die** recording
**Aufzug, der** act (part of play), lift, elevator
**Ausdruck, der** expression
**Ausstattung, die** set
**Beifall, der** applause
**Beleuchter/in, der/die** lighting technician *m/f*
**Beleuchtung, die** lighting
**Besetzung, die** cast
**Betriebsbüro, das** artistic administration
**Betriebsbüroleiter/in, der/die** head of artistic administration *m/f*
**Bezahlung, die** pay
**Bild, das** scene (partition of opera)
**Bodenklappe, die** stage trap door
**Bühne links** stage left
**Bühne rechts** stage right
**Bühne, die** stage
**Bühnenarbeiter/in, der/die** stage hand *m/f*
**Bühnenbild, das** décor, scenery
**Bühnenbildner/in, der/die** scenic designer, set designer *m/f*
**Bühneneingang, der** stage door
**Bühnenmusik, die** incidental music also music played backstage
**Bühnenorchesterprobe, die** *abbr.* **BO** stage orchestral rehearsal
**Bühnenpförtner/in, der/die** stage door man/woman
**Bühnenprobe, die** stage rehearsal
**Bühnentechniker/in, der/die** stage hand *m/f*
**Chor, der** chorus

**Chorbüro, das** chorus office
**Chordirektor, der** chorus master
**Chordirektorin, die** chorus mistress
**darstellen** to interpret, to portray
**Darsteller/in, der/die** interpreter, performer *m/f*
**Darstellung, die** interpretation
**Degen, der** rapier
**Dekoration, die** set
**Dirigent/in, der/die** conductor *m/f*
**Dolch, der** dagger
**Drehbühne, die** revolving stage
**Durchsage, die** announcement
**Einruf, der** stage manager's call
**Eintrittskarte, die** ticket
**eiserne Vorhang, der** fire curtain, safety curtain
**Ensemble, das** company
**Extrachor, der** ad-hoc chorus, extra chorus
**Fach, das** voice type
**Fächer, der** fan (costume prop)
**Fachwechsel, der** voice type change
**Fahrstuhl, der** lift, elevator
**Fan, der** fan (admirer)
**Figur, die** character in the sense of "role"
**Freikarte, die** complimentary ticket
**Gage, die** fee, salary
**Garderobe, die** dressing-room
**Garderobier/e, der/die** dresser *m/f*
**Gastauftritt, der** guest appearance
**gastieren** to guest
**Gastspiel, das** guest appearance
**Gastvertrag, der** guest contract
**Gehalt, das** salary
**Generalmusikdirektor/in, der/die** *abbr.* **GMD** music director *m/f*
**Generalprobe, die** final dress rehearsal

**Gesangslehrer/in, der/die** singing teacher, voice teacher *m/f*
**gestalten** to portray
**Hauptprobe, die** orchestra dress rehearsal
**Honorar, das** fee
**Hosenrolle, die** trouser role
**Inspizient/in, der/die** stage manager *m/f*
**Inspizientenpult, das** stage manager's desk
**Intendant/in, der/die** opera director *m/f*
**Klavierauszug, der** piano score, vocal score
**Klavierhauptprobe, die** piano dress rehearsal
**Korrepetitor/in, der/die** music coach *m/f*
**Kostüm, das** costume
**Kostümabteilung, die** costume department
**Kostümbildner/in, der/die** costume designer *m/f*
**Kostümprobe, die** costume fitting
**Kulisse, die** wings
**Lampenfieber, das** stage fright
**Lautsprecheranlage, die** intercom, loud-speakers, tannoy
**Lebenslauf, der** curriculum vitae (CV), résumé
**Lift, der** lift, elevator
**Luke, die** hatch
**Maske, die** make-up, make-up room
**Maskenbildner/in, der** make-up man/woman
**mitstudieren** to understudy
**Mitstudierende, der/die** understudy
**Möbelabteilung, die** carpenter's shop
**Musihochschule, die** music school
**Musikzimmer, das** music room
**Notenpult, das** music stand
**Opernhaus, das** opera house
**Orchester, das** ochestra
**Orchestergraben, der** orchestra pit
**Orchesterprobe, die** orchestra rehearsal
**Partitur, die** orchestral score
**Pause, die** intermission, interval
**Perücke, die** wig
**Perückenmacher/in, der/die** wig-maker *m/f*
**Pforte, die** stage door

**Pförtner/in, der/die** stage door man/woman
**Phoniater/in, der/die** laryngologist *m/f*
**Premiere, die** opening night
**Probe, die** rehearsal
**Probebühne, die** rehearsal stage
**proben** to rehearse
**Probenplan, der** rehearsal schedule
**Probenraum, der** rehearsal room
**Probenzimmer, das** rehearsal room
**Probesaal, der** rehearsal hall
**Prospekt, der** back cloth
**Publikum, das** audience
**Rauchen verboten** no smoking
**Regieassistent/in, der/die** stage director's assistant *m/f*
**Regisseur/in, der/die** stage director *m/f*
**Repertoire, das** repertoire
**Repetitor/in, der/die** music coach *m/f*
**Requisiten, die** *pl* props, properties
**Requisiteur/in, der/die** prop master *m/f*
**Rolle, die** role
**Rundhorizont, der** cyclorama
**Saalbeleuchtung, die** houselights
**Sänger/in, der/die** singer *m/f*
**Schauspieler/in, der/die** actor/actress
**schauspielern** to act
**Scheinwerfer, der** spot, spotlight
**schmeißen** to fluff your lines
**Schminke, die** make-up
**schminken** to make-up
**Schneider, der** tailor
**Schneiderei, die** costume department
**Schneiderin, die** seamstress
**Schnürboden, der** flies
**Schräge, die** rake (slant of stage floor)
**Schwert, das** sword
**Seitenbühne, die** wings
**Sicherheitsnadel, die** safety pin
**Souffleur/Souffleuse, der/die** prompt, prompter *m/f*
**Souffleurkasten, der** prompt box, prompter's box

# Appendix

soufflieren to prompt
Spesen, die *pl* daily allowance, per diem
Spielplan, der repertory
Spielzeit, die opera season
Statist/in, der/die super, walk-on *m/f*
Statisterie, die supers, walk-ons
Stellprobe, die blocking rehearsal
Stichwort, das cue
Stimmarzt/ärztin, der/die laryngologist *m/f*
Stimme, die voice
Stimmfach, das voice type
Stimmknötchen, die *pl* nodules
Stimmlippen, die *pl* vocal folds
Studienleiter/in, der/die head of musical staff *m/f*
Szene, die scene *partition of opera*
Szenenwechsel, der scene-change
szenische Probe, die staging rehearsal
Tagegeld, das daily allowance, per diem
Theaterkasse, die box office
Tischler/in, der/die carpenter *m/f*
Tischlerei, die carpenter's shop
Ton, der sound
Tontechniker/in, der/die sound technician *m/f*

Umbau, der set change
Ventilator, der fan (for cooling)
Verbeugung, die bow, curtain call, curtsy
Verehrer, der fan (admirer)
Verfolger, der follow-spot
Verfolgungsscheinwerfer, der follow-spot
Versenkung, die lift (movable section of stage)
Versenkungsklappe, die stage trap door
Vertrag, der contract
Verwaltungsdirektor/in, der/die financial manager, head of administration *m/f*
Verwandlung, die scene-change
Vorbühne, die apron (part of stage)
Vorhang, der curtain
vorsingen to audition
Vorsingen, das audition
Vorsingtermin, der audition date, audition time
Vorstellung, die performance
Wiederaufnahme revival production
Zugstange, die fly-bar
Zuschauer, die *pl* audience
Zweitbesetzung, die second cast

# Websites

www.google.de
www.google.com (one of the best search machines)
www.oxfordreference.com (provides for instance *The Concise Oxford Dictionary of Opera Online*)
www.eurail.com

Germany

www.deutschland.de (the official site of Germany)
www.auswaertiges-amt.de (the official site of the Federal Foreign Office, information on the entry into Germany)
www.expatica.com (Living and working in Germany)
www.humboldt-foundation.de/de/programme/betreuung/rat/index.htm (practical hints for your stay in Germany)
www.kulturportal.de (cultural information on Germany, useful link list)
www.hdg.de/lemo/ (German history from 1900 up to the present in the live virtual online museum LeMO)
www.jugendherberge.de (information on youth hostels in Germany)
www.homecompany.de (furnished accommodation)
www.mitwohnzentrale.de (furnished accommodation)
www.immonet.de (furnished accommodation)
www.mifaz.de (lift arranging agency)
www.verkehrsportal.de (driving licenses in Germany)

Studying

www.rektorenkonferenz.de (addresses of all music schools in Germany)
www.campus-germany.de (studying in Germany)
www.das-neue-bafoeg.de/bafoeg_default.htm (financial stipend)
www.istc.org (International Student Identity Card)
www.studentenrabatte.de (discount for students)
www.aimsgraz.org (American Institute of Musical Studies, Graz/Austria)
www.opera-consulting.de
www.opernkurs.de
www.topopera.com
www.wfimc.org (World Federation of International Music Competitions)

# Appendix

**The Business**

www.miz.org (Music Information Centre, *das Musikinformations-zentrum*; all addresses of German music schools and opera houses)

www.buehnengenossenschaft.de (go to *Publikationen*, where you can order *Das Deutsche Bühnenjahrbuch* which contains addresses of agents and opera houses)

www.theaterportal.de

www.buehnenverein.de

www.kuenstlersozialkasse.de

www.versorgungskammer.de (go to *Versorgungsanstalt der deutschen Bühnen* for the information on the additional insurance for singers)

www.musicentral.com/Opera-Singers/

www.theaterjobs.de

**Study Italian**

www.culturaitaliana.it

**Health Care**

www.arts-medicine-europe.org

www.naturalhealthweb.com

www.netdoktor.de

**Chorus work**

www.europachorakademie.de

www.festival-aix.com/academie

www.shmf.de

**Singing and Singers**

www.aria-database.com

www.famiro.de (professional tools for professional singers)

www.gesang.de

www.impresario.ch (opera guide)

www.klassik.com

www.nfcs.net (New Forum for Classical Singers)

www.operabase.com

www.operissimo.com (news on singers and opera houses)

www.orpheus.at

**Periodicals**

www.buehnengenossenschaft.de (chorus jobs)

www.classicalsinger.com

www.nmz.de (Neue Musikzeitung)

www.opernglas.de

www.opernwelt.de

www.operundtanz.de (chorus jobs)

www.orpheusoper.de

# Index

# Appendix

## Credits

Johannes Giebeler, Münster: 174
Roland Halbe, Stuttgart: 23
Wilfried Hösl, München: 28, 66, 73, 78, 80, 161, 165, 166, 183
Thomas Huther, Kassel: 37
Gert Kiermeyer, Halle/Saale: 7

Louis Knobel, Johannesburg/South Africa: 26, 35, 63, 91, 168, 171, 176
Matthias Kolodziej, Freiburg: 86
Paul Leclaire, Köln: 82f.
Diana Rothaug, Kassel: 115
SFF Fotodesign GmbH, Hof: 93

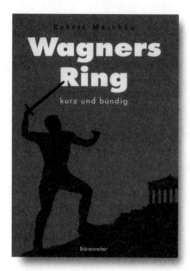